THE MOHICANS OF PARIS

Borgo Press Books by ALEXANDRE DUMAS

Anthony
The Barricade at Clichy; or, The Fall of Napoleon
Bathilda
Caligula
The Corsican Brothers (with Eugène Grangé & Xavier de Montépin)
The Count of Monte Cristo, Part One: The Betrayal of Edmond Dantès
The Count of Monte Cristo, Part Two: The Resurrection of Edmond Dantès
The Count of Monte Cristo, Part Three: The Rise of Monte Cristo
The Count of Monte Cristo, Part Four: The Revenge of Monte Cristo
A Fairy Tale (with Adolphe de Leuven and Léon Lhérie)
The Gold Thieves (with Countess Céleste de Chabrillan)
Kean
The Last of the Three Musketeers; or, The Prisoner of the Bastille
　(Musketeers #3)
Lorenzino
The Mohicans of Paris
Napoléon Bonaparte
Queen Margot
Richard Darlington (with Prosper Dinaux)
Sylvandire
The Three Musketeers (Musketeers #1)
The Three Musketeers—Twenty Years Later (Musketeers #2)
The Tower of Death (with Frédéric Gaillardet)
The Two Dianas (with Paul Meurice)
Urbain Grandier and the Devils of Loudon
The Venetian
The Whites and the Blues
The Widow's Husband; and, Porthos in Search of an Outfit
Young Louix XIV

RELATED DRAMAS:

The Queen's Necklace, by Pierre Decourcelle
The Seed of the Musketeers, by Paul de Kock & Guénée (Musketeers #5)
The San Felice, by Maurice Drack
The Son of Porthos the Musketeer, by Émile Blavet (Musketeers #4)
A Summer Night's Dream, Adolphe de Leuven & Joseph-Bernard Rosier
The Widow's Husband; and, Porthos in Search of an Outfit: Two Dumasian
　Comedies, edited by Frank J. Morlock

THE MOHICANS OF PARIS

A PLAY IN FIVE ACTS

ALEXANDRE DUMAS

Translated and Adapted by Frank J. Morlock

THE BORGO PRESS

MMXIII

THE MOHICANS OF PARIS

FIRST BORGO PRESS EDITION

Published by Wildside Press LLC

www.wildsidebooks.com

DEDICATION

For Conrad Cady

CONTENTS

CAST OF CHARACTERS. 9

PROLOGUE, Scene 1 13

ACT I, Scene 2 .59

ACT I, Scene 3 103

ACT II, Scene 4. 139

ACT III, Scene 5 169

ACT III, Scene 6 207

ACT IV, Scene 7 228

ACT IV, Scene 8 250

ACT V, Scene 9 272

ABOUT THE AUTHOR 293

CAST OF CHARACTERS

Salvator

Mr. Gérard

Philippe Sarranti

Dominique Sarranti

Loredan de Valgeneuse

Monsieur Jackal

Gibassier

Pétrus (Painter)

Jean Robert (Poet)

Ludovic (Doctor)

Sac a Platre (Mason)

Jean Taureau (Carpenter)

Toussaint L'Overture

Henry Bertin, a police commissioner

Cabaret Waiter

Pierre (Waiter)

Police Officer

Pierrot

Polichinelle

Jérôme, a Factor

Jean, a Servant of Mr. Gérard

Croc en Jambes (mute character)

La Gibelotte (mute character)

Rose Noel

La Brocanti

Babolin

Orsola

Suzanne de Valgeneuse

Madame Desmarest

Female Servant of Mr. Gérard

Victor

Leonie

Brésil, Mr. Gérard's dog

PROLOGUE
SCENE 1

A kitchen giving on a park.

Leonie & Brésil resting on a sofa. Orsola entering.

ORSOLA

(aside) Still that child.

(aloud) Go, Leonie, go play in the garden.

LEONIE

(leaving with the dog) Come, Brésil, come.

ORSOLA

(going to Gérard's bedroom and opening the door) He's still sleeping! And this morning, when he wakes, he will, as usual, forget all the promises he made me last night when he was drunk. Truly, I don't know why I give myself so much trouble. I am still young and still pretty while this man—and all this worry for five or six thousand pounds of income! Oh—he owes me a fortune, like the one these miserable children will have one day—playing by the pool. They will have a million and a half each—for taking the trouble to be born while I, after struggling in poverty and shame for fifteen or twenty years arrive at thirty having been the mistress of Mr. Gérard with the immense ambition of becoming the wife of a man of fifty, who the day the thing occurs will be the envy of all the ladies of Viry sur Orge and its environs. Magnificent future indeed worth the trouble of being jealous over.

(Enter postman.)

POSTMAN

(outside) Hey. Anybody home?

ORSOLA

Who's there?

POSTMAN

(entering) Me, the postman, it's a letter.

ORSOLA

Give it here.

POSTMAN

Can't do that!

ORSOLA

Why can't you?

POSTMAN

Because it is for Mr. Gérard.

ORSOLA

Well, Mr. Gérard or me—isn't that the same thing?

POSTMAN

Not quite yet, although they say in town that one day pretty soon it will be. Say, Madame Orsola, the day it happens you'll be a pretty picture!

ORSOLA

Come on, stop the idle talk and give me this letter. Don't you know, I receive all Mr. Gérard's correspondence?

POSTMAN

Yes, but not registered letters which must be signed for.

ORSOLA

(frowning) Look here, Jérôme.

POSTMAN

Madame Orsola?

ORSOLA

I believe that you wish to renew the lease on the little corner house that you rent from Mr. Gérard?

POSTMAN

Certainly, I do.

ORSOLA

Well, you won't, taking this tack with me, I warn you. Good-day, Jérôme, take back your letter.

POSTMAN

Now, now, Madame Orsola, I am not opposed myself to giving you the letter if you would sign in place of Mr. Gérard?

ORSOLA

And why shouldn't I sign in his place?

POSTMAN

Heck, I don't know. Here, here's the register. Only since the letter is for Mr. Gérard, sign "Gérard."

(Orsola takes a pen and signs.)

POSTMAN

(aside) She signed all the same. Oh, she's a real boss-lady.

(aloud) Here's the letter.

(Enter Victor on the stone steps.)

ORSOLA

(aside looking at the letter) A black seal! What does this mean?

VICTOR

Mr. Mailman, do you bring us news of papa?

ORSOLA

(unsealing the letter cautiously) Perhaps!

POSTMAN

Ask Madame Gérard, Monsieur Victor, she's the one who has received the letter.

(Exit postman.)

(Enter Leonie with the hound, Brésil.)

VICTOR

You mean to say "Madame Orsola"—Come Leonie, it's time to take our lesson with Monsieur Sarranti.

(he leaves with his sister and the dog by the door opposite that of Mr. Gérard)

ORSOLA

(alone watching the children leave) Yes, there is news of your father and good! Dead during the crossing! A will.

(the door to the bedroom opens)

Gérard!

(Enter Gérard.)

GÉRARD

(hesitating) What time is it, Orsola?

ORSOLA

Ten o'clock. Wait.

(the clock striking)

GÉRARD

What time did we go to bed?

ORSOLA

Almost midnight.

GÉRARD

And you're up already?

ORSOLA

As usual. Isn't it necessary to take a look over the house in the morning?

GÉRARD

The mistress?

ORSOLA

I am your servant, Monsieur Gérard! And if you please to order I will obey, but meanwhile, I really ought to tell you something—or rather someone is preoccupying me.

GÉRARD

Who?

ORSOLA

This man.

GÉRARD

What man?

ORSOLA

The one your brother imposed as tutor of the children, your Corsican!

GÉRARD

Sarranti!

ORSOLA

Yes!

GÉRARD

And why does he preoccupy you?

ORSOLA

God prevent that no evil befalls us because of him.

GÉRARD

Why do you tell me this?

ORSOLA

First, a man who under your name has deposited one hundred

thousand francs with a notary.

GÉRARD

That proves he has confidence in me, who since he cannot deposit the money in his name deposits it in mine.

ORSOLA

And who, possessing that amount would be content to work for fifteen hundred francs as a tutor to the two children! What these children are to him I cannot say.

GÉRARD

But these children are my brother's and Sarranti has been his friend.

ORSOLA

And today, do you know what your brother's friend is doing?

GÉRARD

What's he doing?

ORSOLA

I am going to tell you, I am, if you don't know, he's a conspirator.

GÉRARD

Sarranti.

ORSOLA

Yes, or I am much deceived. Needless for me to get up at dawn, he's up before me. Then he insists on having the pavilion, doesn't he?

GÉRARD

He's a studious man who likes to work at his ease.

ORSOLA

And one never knows at all with whom or at what he works.

GÉRARD

Oh, I recognize you well in that—always suspicious.

(Enter Jean.)

JEAN

I ask your pardon, sir, to come without being called, but Mr. Sarranti desires to speak to you and you alone—

GÉRARD

Tell him I'll be down.

ORSOLA

No, tell him to come up.

GÉRARD

(after looking at Orsola) Yes, let him come up.

JEAN

I'll go do it, sir.

(Jean exits.)

GÉRARD

Now, Orsola, if you would leave us.

ORSOLA

Ah, then you have got secrets from me?

GÉRARD

No, but Mr. Sarranti's secrets are not mine but his.

ORSOLA

With your permission, Monsieur Gérard, the secrets of Sarranti are ours or he can keep his secrets.

GÉRARD

Here's Sarranti.

ORSOLA

(hiding in a cabinet) I warn you, I am listening.

(Sarranti enters.)

SARRANTI

(looking around) Are we alone, my friend? Can I speak in

complete confidence?

GÉRARD

We are alone and you can speak.

SARRANTI

Above all, dear Mr. Gérard, I must assure you of one thing: it's that all I am going to say to you was known to your brother from the first day I saw him, so that he knew perfectly well that it was to a conspirator that he opened his door to, when he charged me with the education of his children.

GÉRARD

Why, is it true that you conspire?

SARRANTI

Alas yes, Mr. Gérard, but be easy, I've taken every precaution not to compromise you. In two words, here are the facts. A conspiracy is organized; today at four o'clock, it goes off. I cannot tell you who the leaders are, their secret is not mine. What I can tell you, what I can swear to you is that the most illustrious names will try to ruin the government.

GÉRARD

How unfortunate!

SARRANTI

Will we succeed? Will we fail? If we succeed, we will be acclaimed as heroes—if we miscarry—the scaffold awaits us.

GÉRARD

The scaffold.

SARRANTI

One more time. Don't fear of being compromised. Here is a letter that I address to you as if no confidence had been placed in you and in which I recount that important business calls me to leave you. If the conspiracy fails, I will save myself if I can— now will you help me to the end? Give me Jean who is a faithful servant—let him keep two saddled horses for me all day with the hundred thousand francs in the saddlebags that I confided in you and that you have withdrawn from the notary. The whole length of the route to Nantes I have helpers who will hide me. At Nantes I will embark for the Indies.

GÉRARD

You won't find my brother there because three months ago I received a letter from him in which he announced that, his fortune having reached the figure he desired, he was starting on his way back to us.

SARRANTI

No, but I will find another friend there, General Premont. Now dear Monsieur Gérard, you hold my life in your hands. Don't rush to reply. I am going to my apartment to burn all the papers that could compromise me and in five minutes I will return to learn your response.

(going to leave) No need to tell you who this secret must be kept from.

(Gérard replies by a motion of his head. Sarranti goes off. Orsola enters from the cabinet.)

GÉRARD

Have you heard, Orsola?

ORSOLA

All!

GÉRARD

What's to be done?

ORSOLA

Do what he asks.

GÉRARD

What—you whom I've always found to be the enemy of Sarranti?

ORSOLA

I say you must give him Jean. I tell you you must keep two horses ready and pray to God or rather the Devil, that he fails— for never will a like occasion present itself to make us million- aires.

GÉRARD

Millionaires—what are you raving about?

ORSOLA

Nothing. Work on one thing at a time. It is to take back your counter-letter. Me, I am going to send it before any time is lost. I'll take care of the rest.

GÉRARD

What do you mean "the rest"?

ORSOLA

Ah, that's right. You don't know yet. Read this letter, which just came for you this morning. Here it is. Read it after he leaves.

(Orsola exits crossing in front of Sarranti)

(Enter Sarranti.)

SARRANTI

Well, dear Gérard, have you thought about it?

GÉRARD

Jean is at your disposition. The horses will be saddled and waiting for you with the money in the saddlebags.

SARRANTI

Fine! Here's your letter. From today I regard myself as having the hundred thousand crowns returned since the money has been withdrawn from the notary. I cannot return through Viry and if I am neither taken prisoner nor killed, a word from me will tell you where to hold my money.

GÉRARD

It will be done point for point according to your wishes, dear

Monsieur Sarranti.

SARRANTI

Monsieur Gérard count on my eternal recognition. Till we meet again. Perhaps goodbye!

(Exit Sarranti.)

GÉRARD

What did Orsola mean, "Never a better chance for us to become millionaires?" This woman never does anything without reason—This letter bordered in black that she left me in parting and told me to read—it carries a stamp from Marseille. Ah—I am not the first to open it. A second hidden sheet. My brother's signature. "This is my holographic will." Jacques is dead.

(Gérard falls into an armchair. Orsola appears slowly climbing the steps outside the house, and while Gérard reads, comes without being seen nor heard to peer over the back of his armchair.)

GÉRARD

Let's see the letter first.

(reading the letter) "To Monsieur Gérard, proprietor at Viry sur Orge" indeed, it's for me. "Monsieur, I have sad news to announce to you. Your brother Jacques embarked aboard La Mouette, merchant brig from Marseille under my command, took a pernicious fever, and in passing the Cape of Good Hope died at the latitude of Saint Helena, 12 June last, at five o'clock. He left a will in duplicate, the original to be taken to his notary, Mr. Barrateau, Rue de Bac #31, the other to be sent to you, so that you will know directly the dispositions he took. His last words in expiring were, 'My God, care for my children.' With regret at being the bearer of such bad news, I am, etc., Captain Lucas." His last words were, "My God, care for my children."

(He remains motionless.)

ORSOLA

Let's see—read the rest.

GÉRARD

(jumping) You were there, you!

ORSOLA

Yes.

GÉRARD

(reading) "At sea, 1st of January 1820, sensing that my illness is mortal, and that it pleases the all-powerful Lord to recall me to him, I intend, being in full possession of my faculties, to divide my fortune between my sole remaining relatives, my good brother, Gérard, and my dear children, Victor and Leonie. This division is simple. I leave one and a half million to each of my children. I desire that save for the expense of their education and upbringing, the revenue of this three million shall accumulate until their majority; it is to my brother, Gérard, that I have given charge of watching over them."

(he stops a moment and wipes his face) "As to him, I know the simplicity of his tastes, I leave to him his choice of a sum of three hundred thousand or an annual income of twenty-four thousand francs a year. If one of my children dies, I want his share to be given to the survivor—if both die—"

(stopping) Oh!

ORSOLA

Keep on, what's so astonishing that both might die?

GÉRARD

(continuing in a trembling voice) "If the two children were to die, my brother shall become the sole heir."

ORSOLA

(low voice) The sole heir.

(louder) You understand, Gérard?

GÉRARD

Yes, but they will live.

ORSOLA

Who knows—children are so fragile!

GÉRARD

My poor brother.

ORSOLA

What do you want? You must support with courage these misfortunes that you cannot combat. Death is one of those misfortunes. Today, his turn, tomorrow ours.

GÉRARD

Yes, I know that quite well. My brother was nothing to you, you never saw him, and then—are you happy, ambitious one?— these are our riches!

ORSOLA

We—rich?

GÉRARD

Certainly, since my poor brother left us three hundred thousand francs.

ORSOLA

You call that being rich?

GÉRARD

Without doubt.

ORSOLA

It's the children who are rich—three million!

GÉRARD

Orsola! Orsola!

ORSOLA

What?

(Jean enters.)

JEAN

Monsieur Gérard, the two horses are saddled; but it remains for you to give me what is in the suitcases.

GÉRARD

That's right.

(low, to Orsola) You know what it's about?

ORSOLA

Several hundred thousand shillings.

GÉRARD

And you are still of the opinion I should give them to him?

ORSOLA

To the last sou!

GÉRARD

(going to his desk) Wait Jean—take one of these sacks. I will take the other!

(to Orsola) You understand, I intend—

ORSOLA

Go! Go! The air will make you feel better. You are pale as a cadaver.

GÉRARD

(after looking at Orsola) Come Jean! Come!

(He goes out.)

ORSOLA

Oh—debate with yourself as much as you like. I am like one of our mountain bears—I hold you between my claws. You will not escape me.

(looking out the window) Cursed children—whom I've always detested from instinct. There they are. They're playing at the side of the lake. Victor unties his boat and makes Leonie get up. The dog follows them to the shore and when I think that if the boat capsized. It's true the dog is there. First I must get rid of the dog.

GÉRARD

(outside) Victor! Victor!

VICTOR

Uncle?

GÉRARD

I've already forbidden you to go out in the boat because you don't know how to steer it. Look, you see, your sister almost fell in the water.

ORSOLA

(to Gérard) Oh, let the children alone; they are having fun.

(aside) He never forgets to take precautions against good luck—the imbecile.

(Gérard enters.)

GÉRARD

That's done with. Now, Sarranti can come.

ORSOLA

Did the air make you feel any better?

GÉRARD

Admit that you read this will and letter before I did?

ORSOLA

Well, since it was there—have I committed a crime?

GÉRARD

My poor brother.

(He puts his handkerchief to his eyes.)

ORSOLA

Bah!—you know the song of our mountains.

Happiness is for the Gods
Who leave pleasure to men
Bless the dead who are in heaven
But console the hearts of those
Who remain on Earth where we are.

GÉRARD

Shut up! Shut up! To sing at such a moment is impious.

ORSOLA

Impious? Get out.

GÉRARD

From charity leave me alone for a while.

ORSOLA

Oh, I ask nothing better. You are not very gay company.

(going, singing)

The dead in their graves
Feel neither cold nor hunger.

(Gérard closes the door after her.)

GÉRARD

Oh, this woman is my evil genius.

(Enter Victor followed by the dog, Brésil.)

VICTOR

Here I am, uncle.

GÉRARD

Victor.

VICTOR

You see I am good and I obey you carefully.

GÉRARD

Yes, you are a good little child.

VICTOR

Then hug me, my good uncle.

GÉRARD

(aside) His good uncle.

VICTOR

My sister can pick some flowers, right?

GÉRARD

As many as she likes.

VICTOR

The postman came this morning—did he bring news about papa?

GÉRARD

(hesitating) No, my child, why?

VICTOR

Oh, it's because Madame Orsola received a big letter outlined in black.

(Gérard chokes) What's wrong, uncle?

GÉRARD

(rising) Nothing, my child, nothing.

(He goes into his room.)

VICTOR

It's funny. You would say my uncle is crying. I always thought only children cried.

ORSOLA

(outside) Leonie! Have you already finished picking my flowers?

LEONIE

These flowers are not for you, they are for my uncle.

VICTOR

(at the window) And my uncle just told me that my sister can pick all she wants.

ORSOLA

It is possible that your uncle said that, but I say otherwise.

VICTOR

Pick away, Leonie! You don't have to take orders except from my uncle.

ORSOLA

Take care, Leonie.

LEONIE

Of what?

ORSOLA

Of making me come down—for it you make me come down, you will have it out with me.

LEONIE

Come then, nasty woman.

ORSOLA

(rushing towards the garden) Devil's child.

VICTOR

You know that if you touch my sister, Brésil is there!

(noise of a little girl screaming; Brésil jumps through the window) Uncle! Uncle!

GÉRARD

(entering) What is wrong, my God?

VICTOR

It's that mean Orsola who is beating Leonie because she's picking some flowers. Didn't you permit Leonie to pick the flowers—do they belong to Madame Orsola?

GÉRARD

Orsola! Orsola!

ORSOLA

Here I am—sir!

(She shows Gérard her bloody arm.)

GÉRARD

Who did that to you?

ORSOLA

Brésil! I hope you will punish your niece and you will kill the dog.

VICTOR

Why kill Brésil? He was protecting his mistress—and you were beating her. Brésil was doing his duty.

GÉRARD

Victor, go put Brésil on his chain.

VICTOR

I am going, uncle, but you won't kill Brésil will you?

GÉRARD

No, child—rest easy.

VICTOR

Oh! Oh!

(Victor goes out.)

ORSOLA

On the contrary, they will caress him, the poor animal! What's he done? He's murdered Orsola. What's Orsola? A serving maid to be thrown out the door when one is angry with her. But she won't wait to be kicked out, this servant, she's going by herself. Goodbye, sir.

GÉRARD

Orsola, where are you going?

ORSOLA

I'm going to find a master who will do right by me—and a dog who won't murder me.

GÉRARD

Come on, let me see! The blood is flowing, but the wound is not dangerous.

ORSOLA

You would much prefer if I had a broken arm, right?

GÉRARD

Listen, Orsola; Sarranti has gone. We will part from the children. We will put them in a pension.

ORSOLA

Oh, if I stay here, I will take care of the children.

GÉRARD

Why not stay here? You know very well, I cannot do without you. What do you lack here? The right to command? You have. For fifteen years, you've called yourself Madame Gérard. Look, Orsola, today is a day from the devil—sad as it is don't make it terrible.

ORSOLA

Oh! You know how much influence you have over me.

DOMINIQUE

(in the garden) Mr. Gérard! Mr. Gérard!

GÉRARD

Listen, isn't someone calling me?

(Dominique Sarranti in lay costume.)

DOMINIQUE

(entering quickly) Mr. Gérard! Aren't you Mr. Gérard?

GÉRARD

Yes. What do you want from me?

DOMINIQUE

Have you seen my father? I am the son of Mr. Sarranti. They just came to my home to arrest him. They are pursuing him like a conspirator.

GÉRARD

I hear the gallop of a horse.

DOMINIQUE

Ah! There he is.

SARRANTI

(entering, covered with dust) Dominique here! So much the better. I can embrace you at last.

DOMINIQUE

(jumping on his neck) Father.

SARRANTI

The conspiracy is discovered. I have to flee. Is all ready?

DOMINIQUE

Father, I am going with you.

SARRANTI

No, no! You will compromise yourself uselessly.

DOMINIQUE

What difference?

SARRANTI

You would compromise us. Betrayed! Denounced! Ah the wretches! A plot so well constructed, a conspiracy so well set up.

DOMINIQUE

Then flee right now; flee without waiting; your safety above all!

SARRANTI

And you, return to Paris; take a detour so none know you've come—my security, the peace of Mr. Gérard depends on it.

ORSOLA

(aside) Fine. We will be alone.

GÉRARD

(calling) Jean, the horses.

JEAN

They are ready, sir.

DOMINIQUE

Leave, leave, Father.

SARRANTI

Goodbye!

(to his son) Come!

(to Gérard) My friend, between us—it's life and death.

DOMINIQUE

(pulling him) Well, come then!

GÉRARD

Be careful!

SARRANTI

Oh—don't worry. I am well armed. They won't take me alive.

(He leaves with Dominique.)

GÉRARD

Fatal day.

ORSOLA

(preparing the table) On the contrary—happy day.

GÉRARD

What are you doing?

ORSOLA

It's four in the afternoon, and you've had nothing all day.

GÉRARD

I'm not hungry—I won't eat—I'm suffocated.

ORSOLA

Oh go on! People say that every time they feel sad and they always end by eating. Get some strength.

GÉRARD

Yes, I know that what you want me to do requires strength.

ORSOLA

Drink this glass of Madeira, first.

(Gérard drinks while Orsola goes out to prepare the table.)

GÉRARD

I don't know what this woman mixes in my drinks; this isn't wine I've just had—it's liquid fire.

(Orsola returns with two plates) Why do you bring two places?

ORSOLA

Because we are dining tête-à-tête.

GÉRARD

But the children.

ORSOLA

Let them be served on the lawn. As they have no liking for me, they will prefer that.

GÉRARD

Who will serve them?

ORSOLA

The gardener; I already told him; after which he leaves for Morsang.

GÉRARD

It's five leagues from here to Morsang.

ORSOLA

Also—he won't be back until tomorrow.

GÉRARD

And what's he going to do at Morsang?

ORSOLA

An errand.

GÉRARD

For whom?

ORSOLA

For me—can I not give an errand to the gardener?

GÉRARD

Surely—but then the house will be empty.

ORSOLA

(giving him a glass) That's what's necessary.

GÉRARD

Why this glass?

ORSOLA

Didn't you ask me for a drink?

GÉRARD

No.

ORSOLA

I thought—

(She wishes to take the glass back.)

GÉRARD

Give it to me! When once I've had this cursed wine—and why must the house be empty?

ORSOLA

I'll tell you when the moment comes.

(she lets a plate fall—it breaks) When we are millionaires, we will eat in the money.

(she picks up the pieces and throws them in a corner) And if the plates break at least the pieces will be expensive.

GÉRARD

Millionaires! Never!

(He rises and intends to go to his room.)

ORSOLA

What are you doing? What are you doing? Sit down there.

(She forces him to sit before a full glass.)

GÉRARD

My throat is dry. My mouth is burning.

ORSOLA

Drink then.

GÉRARD

Orsola, why is it that having had hardly half a bottle, my head is swimming, and what I see runs with blood.

ORSOLA

Really, Gérard, you are not a man.

GÉRARD

No, it's true. A man has his reason, a man has his free will, a man says to himself, "God forbids doing evil" and doesn't do it. Where as I—

ORSOLA

Well—you?

GÉRARD

No, I am a brute, an animal without understanding, a ferocious beast. Is it blood or wine you've given me to drink? I am thirsty.

ORSOLA

Drink then.

(Gérard empties a glass of wine, fills it, and wants to empty a second) Enough—you won't be good for anything.

GÉRARD

Yes, you know quite well that now you can propose what you wish and that I am ready for anything.

ORSOLA

Are you sure?

GÉRARD

(holding his head between his hands) Oh!

ORSOLA

You've figured out what we are going to do, right?

GÉRARD

(rising and calling) William! William!

ORSOLA

What do you want?

GÉRARD

I see it clearly. I am calling the gardener.

ORSOLA

To do what?

GÉRARD

To take the children away.

ORSOLA

Come on. I thought it was agreed.

(aside) I was mistaken. He hasn't had enough to drink.

(aloud) Millionaire—you understand, millionaire!

GÉRARD

O serpent with the face of a woman.

(He drinks and passes violently to stupidity.)

(Orsola opens the desk which the money was kept. Then with a scissors, she breaks the lock.)

ORSOLA

There—it's better this way.

GÉRARD

What is better?

ORSOLA

You understand. It will be better if it seems Sarranti committed the act.

GÉRARD

What act?

ORSOLA

You don't understand?

GÉRARD

No.

ORSOLA

Sarranti came yesterday to steal from you the sum your notary brought you;—to steal it he forced the secretary, when he was doing it, the children entered by chance and so as not to be denounced by them, he killed them. Do you understand now?

GÉRARD

(drunk) Yes, I understand, but he will deny it.

ORSOLA

He will return to deny it? Does he dare to return to France where he will be condemned as a conspirator, as a thief, and an assassin?

GÉRARD

No, he wouldn't dare.

ORSOLA

Beside, we will be millionaires; and one can do many things with three millions.

GÉRARD

But how will we be millionaires?

ORSOLA

Since you take care of the little boy, and I take care of the little
girl.

GÉRARD

(recoiling with fear) I didn't say that! I didn't say that.

ORSOLA

You said it.

GÉRARD

Never! Never! Ah, my poor Victor.

(Enter Victor and Leonie holding each other by the hand.)

VICTOR

You called me, Uncle?

ORSOLA

Yes, your uncle wanted to know if the gardener is still here.

VICTOR

No, he left, and he has closed the gate to the park.

(Orsola goes into Gérard's room.)

GÉRARD

(follow her with eyes full of terror) Where are you going?

ORSOLA

(from the room) You are going to find out!

GÉRARD

(looking at the children) Oh, if I take the two of them in my arms and if I escape with them.

(Orsola returns with Gérard's rifle and gives it to him.)

GÉRARD

What is that?

ORSOLA

You can see quite well.

(She puts the rifle into his hands.)

VICTOR

Oh—Uncle, are you going to shoot something?

ORSOLA

Yes, we are going to have a lot of company tomorrow, so it's necessary for your uncle to kill a little game.

VICTOR

Oh, I am going with you, Uncle, may I go with you?

(He runs ahead.)

GÉRARD

No—no.

ORSOLA

Well—decide, coward, you know very well by tomorrow there will be no more time.

VICTOR

(outside) Come, Uncle.

ORSOLA

Do you hear that child calling you? But go with him then since he's the one who wants it.

(She pushes Gérard out.)

LEONIE

(stamping her foot) I want to go with my brother, I want to go!

ORSOLA

Go to your room, Miss.

LEONIE

I will go without you, thanks.

(She leaves.)

ORSOLA

(alone—night has fallen) The hour has come. Riches and vengeance at once. They are going to pay for all the humiliations these cursed children have caused me for the past four years—so long as he doesn't lose heart.

(looks out the window) What's he doing? Getting in the boat with the child. He crossed the lake. Ah, I understand. The noise of the rifle worries him. He prefers—the coward.

VICTOR

(in the garden) Oh, Uncle, what are you doing? My good Uncle. I have never done wrong to anybody. My good Uncle, don't murder me.

LEONIE

(in her room) They are killing my brother! Help! Help!

ORSOLA

(rushing into the room) You will shut up, wretch!

(The stage remains empty.)

VICTOR

Uncle—my good uncle! Ah!

(The furious snarling of the dog who breaks his chains and who comes on stage dragging his chain.)

LEONIE

(in her room) Help—help! Brésil! Brésil!

(The dog hurtles through the door breaking a bottle—disappearing into the room.)

ORSOLA

(in the room) Cursed dog.

(she screams) Ah!

(Gérard appears in the rear, pale, eyes haggard, his rifle in his hands. Silence on all sides.)

GÉRARD

Oh, wretch or infamous creature that I am. Oh, this voice, this prayer - it will pursue me through eternity. My God, I guess I dared pronounce the name of the Lord. And the other, the other who cried inside. No, I cannot remain another minute in this house. I want to flee. I want to leave France. Let us flee! Orsola! Orsola!

ORSOLA

(in the room) Help! Help! I'm dying.

(Leonie can be seen escaping through the window.)

GÉRARD

Orsola! It's Orsola who is dying who calls for help! Orsola—

(he opens the door of the room) What his happened then?

(He goes in and returns with a wounded Orsola.)

ORSOLA

(hand to her throat) The dog! The dog!

(She falls dying.)

GÉRARD

Strangled! Justice of heaven! And I, to what am I reserved, if this woman has received such a punishment? And Leonie, where is she? Escaped without doubt. It's a fire in my brain. I am going mad!

(falls in an armchair) But if she has escaped she will speak; she will denounce us.

(jumping towards Orsola) Why did you allow her to flee? Speak! Speak! Dead! She is dead! Some air! Some air!

(he tears his shirt and tie) I am suffocating.

(falling on his knees, his arms extended toward the window) Some air!

(suddenly his look becomes fixed) What do I see down there? The dog! The dog! What's he doing? He's turning around the lake. He's following the same route we took. He's plunging in. He reappears in the water. There he is. What's he dragging after him—the body! Horror! We are at the day of the last judgment. The abyss surrenders its dead.

(he grabs his rifle and fires at the dog) Dead! Good. Leonie now. I must find Leonie again.

(He hurries out of the room.)

CURTAIN

ACT I
SCENE 2

At Bornier's (in La Halle).

Jean Taureau and others. A pierrot sleeping on a table.

JEAN TAUREAU

(striking the table with a bottle) Some wine! Some wine! Wine!

WAITER

Here's the wine you asked for.

JEAN TAUREAU

I see the wine but I don't see the cards.

WAITER

As for the cards, you must be in your mourning, Mr. Jean Taureau, because you know very well no one gives cards at these hours.

TOUSSAINT

And the reason?

WAITER

Because it is forbidden by the regulations.

JEAN TAUREAU

What are your regulations to me?

WAITER

To you, nothing, but something to us.

SAC A PLATRE

But then if one cannot gamble, what do you want to do with us in your place?

WAITER

Fine. No one is forcing you to stay, Mr. Sac a Platre.

JEAN TAUREAU

Ah, indeed! Do you know you appear to me to have a pretty comic air. Hell's bells! Some cards or with a blow I will demolish the place.

WAITER

No one's afraid of you, Jean Taureau though you may be.

(Enter Pétrus, Jean Robert, Ludovic.)

PÉTRUS

Here we are!

LUDOVIC

The cabaret appears to you sufficiently sleazy?

JEAN ROBERT

I could find it even if I were blind.

PÉTRUS

In that case, let's go in.

JEAN ROBERT

Are you sure?

PÉTRUS

Why not?

JEAN ROBERT

Because it is always time to stop when youth goes to embark on stupidity.

LUDOVIC

A stupidity—in what?

JEAN ROBERT

By God, in that instead of going to supper tranquilly, or to Verys or to the Rock or to the Provincial Brothers, you want to spend the night in an ignoble hole where we will drink from the infusion of logwood in place of wine of Bordeaux, and where we'll eat cat instead of wild rabbit.

SAC A PLATRE

Do you hear, Jean Taureau? He said a hole.

TOUSSAINT

He said logwood.

SAC A PLATRE

He said "some cat."

JEAN TAUREAU

Let him say it. He who laughs best, laughs last.

LUDOVIC

Do what you please, gentlemen, but me, I declare that I didn't get an invitation to dine at Bordier's this evening. I am here and here I sup.

PÉTRUS

As for me, in my capacity as painter, I who have not always had wine from logwood to drink or even a cat to eat, I who frequently have models of both sexes, types of living cadavers that, unlike the dead, have inferior souls, I who have slept in a hole belonging to a bear or the lair of lions, throwing myself with the quadrupeds when I hadn't even three francs to go home to Papa Cadmoor or Miss Rosive, the blond, I am not disgusted, and I agree with Ludovic and I say: I am staying.

JEAN ROBERT

My dear Pétrus—you are only half drunk, but you are completely

Gascon.

PÉTRUS

Gascon! Right! I am from Saint Lo. If there are Gascons at Saint
Lo, there are Normands at Tarbes.

JEAN ROBERT

Well, I say to you, Gascon from St. Lo, you boast some faults
that you haven't got to hide the qualities which you possess.
You act the rake for fear of appearing naive. You pretend to
be wicked for fear of blushing to appear good. You've never
entered a lion's den or a bear's cave, you've never put foot in a
cabaret in La Halle, any more than Ludovic, any more than I,
any more than the young people who respect themselves or the
workers who toil.

SAC A PLATRE

Good! So we don't work, I suppose?

JEAN TAUREAU

But let them talk.

PÉTRUS

Have you finished your sermon? In that case, so be it.

(He yawns.)

TOUSSAINT

Do you understand a word they are saying?

SAC A PLATRE

Not a traitorous word!

JEAN ROBERT

(continuing) Then you want to sup in a rug. Let us sup, my friend, that at least will have a result; it will disgust you for the rest of your life.

(striking the table with his switch)

Boy!

WAITER

(from below) Coming, sir, coming.

JEAN ROBERT

Look, there's a menu, make your choice. We will be like princes here.

LUDOVIC

Yes, all we lack is breathable air.

PÉTRUS

Good. Have them open a window.

(A Polichinelle enters and goes to a sleeping Pierrot.)

POLICHINELLE

Hey! Vol-au-Vent!

PIERROT

Is it you? And Mr. Jackal?

POLICHINELLE

He will be here at two in the morning. That's the time for the rendezvous.

(Pierrot leaves. Polichinelle sits down. Let's his head fall on the table and appears to sleep.)

LUDOVIC

(to Jean Robert) Have you seen?

JEAN ROBERT

What?

LUDOVIC

(pointing with his head) There!

JEAN ROBERT

Yes.

LUDOVIC

It's comic.

JEAN ROBERT

No. There are men on the lookout for some thief. We are in what they call a mousetrap—Boy!

WAITER

(entering)

(looking at Polichinelle) Huh, I thought it was a Pierrot but it's a Polichinelle. I was mistaken. What do you want, gentlemen?

JEAN ROBERT

(to Pétrus) Have you finished with the menu?

PÉTRUS

Yes—six dozen oysters, six muttonchops, and an omelette.

WAITER

And some wine, gentlemen—what kind?

PÉTRUS

Three Chablis—the best—with seltzer water if there is some in this establishment.

WAITER

And some fine stuff, rest assured, you will be served.

PÉTRUS

(retaining the waiter) One moment, young man! Whose voice was that I heard, accompanied by a drum that I noticed on the first floor?

WAITER

It's the little gypsy! Rose Noel, pupil of Brocanti.

PÉTRUS

What a coincidence, a gypsy! And here I was, dreaming of a picture of Mignon! Is she young, your gypsy?

WAITER

Fifteen.

PÉTRUS

Pretty?

VICTOR

I think so—but you know—

PÉTRUS

What?

WAITER

She's forbidden fruit.

PÉTRUS

So much the better. You will bring her for dessert. Here's a crown for her.

WAITER

Oh well, yes, for her—you mean for Brocanti?

PÉTRUS

That's not my concern. I am giving a crown. No matter in whose pocket it falls.

SAC A PLATRE

Six dozen oysters, six mutton chops, an omelette, three chablis—the best, seltzer water if there is any—a gypsy for dessert, even if there isn't any. Nice. We have an affair with these fops.

TOUSSAINT

With these sons of the wealthy.

PÉTRUS

(going to the window and opening it) And now let us get rid of the carbonic acid! Yuck!

JEAN TAUREAU

Excuse me! These gentlemen are opening the window or so it appears.

PÉTRUS

As you see, my dear friend.

JEAN TAUREAU

First of all, I am not your friend, since I don't know you from

Adam or Eve. Close the window!

PÉTRUS

What's your name, sir, if you please?

JEAN TAUREAU

I am called John Bull—since I can kill a bull with a single blow of my hand.

PÉTRUS

This last detail is useless and I don't want to know your name. Now that I know it, Mr. Jean Taureau, or John Bull, here is my friend Dr. Ludovic, a distinguished physician, who is going to explain to you briefly what the air must consist of to be breathable.

JEAN TAUREAU

What do I care what the air consists of?

LUDOVIC

He's saying, Mr. Jean Taureau, that for the atmosphere not to be noxious to the lungs of an honest man, it must be composed of seventy-nine parts nitrogen and twenty-one parts oxygen, and of a certain quantity of dissolved water—the quantity varies according to the climate and temperature—for example in Senegal.

SAC A PLATRE

Say, Jean Taureau, I think he's talking Latin.

JEAN TAUREAU

Good! I am going to make him speak French, I am.

SAC A PLATRE

And if he doesn't understand?

JEAN TAUREAU

(showing two fists) They kill.

(he takes three steps forward) Go—close the window! And be quick about it.

PÉTRUS

(turning his back to the window and crossing his arms) Perhaps that's your opinion, Mr. Jean Taureau, but it isn't mine.

JEAN TAUREAU

What! It isn't yours? You mean you have an opinion? You?

PÉTRUS

And why cannot a man have an opinion when a brute pretends to have one?

JEAN TAUREAU

Say, my friends, do you think this unlucky fop is calling me a brute?

SAC A PLATRE

Damn! That's what I think.

JEAN TAUREAU

Well—what's to be done?

TOUSSAINT

He must be made to close the window first—because it's your opinion—and then kill him.

JEAN TAUREAU

Fine! Now you're talking.

(to the young men) Thunder! Get going. Close the window.

PÉTRUS

There's neither thunder nor lightning. The window is staying open.

JEAN ROBERT

Let's see, Pétrus.

(to Jean Taureau)

Sir, we have just come from outside, and coming in this room we have been suffocated by the change in the temperature. Permit us to leave the window open for a short while to refresh the air—then we will close it.

JEAN TAUREAU

You opened it without my permission.

PÉTRUS

Well?

JEAN TAUREAU

You must ask permission. Perhaps you would have received it.

PÉTRUS

That's it, enough. I opened the window because it pleases me, and it will remain open so long as it pleases me.

JEAN ROBERT

Shut up, Pétrus.

PÉTRUS

(half laughing, half threatening) No, I won't shut up. If the gentleman's called Jean Taureau, I am called Pierre Herbel de Courtney—and I am not accustomed to being led around by clowns like this.

(At the word "clowns," five men rise and take a step forward.)

JEAN ROBERT

Before fighting, let's see if we can have an explanation; after that it will be too late.

(rising in his turn) What do these gentlemen want?

JEAN TAUREAU

He's still insulting us; he calls us gentlemen!

SAC A PLATRE

We are not gentlemen, understand?

PÉTRUS

You are right, you are not gentlemen, you are rednecks.

SAC A PLATRE

They call us rednecks. Oh, there it is. They give us out as
rednecks.

TOUSSAINT

(separating from the others) But let me pass—

JEAN TAUREAU

Shut up—all stay where you are—this is my concern.

SAC A PLATRE

Why's it your concern more than mine?

JEAN TAUREAU

First of all—because there's no need for five against three when
one suffices. To your seat, Sac a Platre. To your seat, Croc en
Jambes.

(they take seats) That's better. And now my little loves—let's sing that song again—first verse. Do you intend to close the window?

THE THREE YOUNG MEN

No!

JEAN TAUREAU

(exasperated) Then you want me to pulverize you?

JEAN ROBERT

Try!

PÉTRUS

Get out of the way, Jean Robert. This is my affair.

JEAN ROBERT

(pushing him away softly) Keep the others in respect, you and Ludovic—I will take care of this one.

(He puts his finger on Jean Taureau's breast.)

JEAN TAUREAU

(frowning) I believe you are speaking of me, my prince?

JEAN ROBERT

Of you yourself!

JEAN TAUREAU

And to what do I owe the honor of being chosen by you?

JEAN ROBERT

I might say that being the most insolent you deserve the rudest lesson—but that's not the motive.

JEAN TAUREAU

I am waiting for the motive.

JEAN ROBERT

It's that having the same first name, we are naturally alike. You are called Jean Taureau, and I am called Jean Robert.

JEAN TAUREAU

It's true, I am called Jean Taureau, but you are called Jean—

JEAN ROBERT

You lie!

(Hits him in the eye. Jean Taureau takes three steps back and falls on a table which he breaks in two. Pétrus trips up Sac a Platre and rolls him near Jean Taureau. Ludovic whacks Toussaint, who falls in the lap of Croc en Jambes whose hands are at his side.)

POLICHINELLE

(raising his head) Bam!

(He falls back to sleep.)

JEAN ROBERT

Round one.

JEAN TAUREAU

(heavily) That's what happens when you are taken unawares; a child will beat you.

JEAN ROBERT

Well, this time, take your time, Jean Taureau, for my intention is to break you in pieces like the table.

JEAN TAUREAU

We are going to see.

(fist raised, he stalks towards Jean Robert, who takes the carpenter's blow on his arm and with a half turn, kicks Jean Taureau in the chest who falls in the chimney)

JEAN TAUREAU

Oof!

POLICHINELLE

(rising) Bam!

(He goes back to sleep.)

TOUSSAINT and SAC A PLATRE

To knives. To knives.

JEAN TAUREAU

Well, since they are forcing us—to knives!

JEAN ROBERT

Then to barricades.

(The waiter comes in carrying the oysters.)

WAITER

Wow! It seems it is not the time.

(puts the oysters on the table) Help! Help!

(He leaves running.)

MR. JACKAL

(appearing at the door dressed like a Turk) Oh, that's all. They said someone was being strangled here.

(to Polichinelle) Give me your place and leave quickly.

POLICHINELLE

Why, is that you, Mr. Jackal?

MR. JACKAL

Hush!

POLICHINELLE

(giving up his seat) Bam!

(He leaves.)

JEAN TAUREAU (and his companions)

To knives! To knives!

MASKS

Bravo! We are going to laugh!

(The young men take their tables and form a barricade. Pétrus tears a stick from the curtain. Ludovic brings the oysters into the fortifications.)

LUDOVIC

Some snacks and some projectiles.

(He throws the shells at his adversary.)

JEAN TAUREAU

Let me pulverize the guy in black!

(He pulls his carpenter's compass from his pocket.)

JEAN ROBERT

(jumping over the table, switch in his hand) But you still haven't had enough.

MASKS

Bravo! Bravo! The guy in black!

JEAN TAUREAU

No, I won't have enough until I've put six inches of my compass
in your torso.

JEAN ROBERT

Meaning, not being the strongest you are the most treacherous!
Since you cannot win, you intend to murder.

JEAN TAUREAU

Thunder! I intend to avenge myself.

JEAN ROBERT

(his little switch in his hand)

Take care, Jean Taureau, for on my honor you have never before
run such a danger as the one you are running now.

(to the crowd) My friends, you are men—make this fellow listen
to reason, you can see I am calm and he is out of his head.

JEAN TAUREAU

(escaping from those who wish to calm him down) Oh! I have
never run such a danger as I now run? Do you intend to protect
yourself with that switch against my compass?

JEAN ROBERT

You are deceived, John Bull! For my cane is not a cane, it's a viper and if you doubt it, there—see its fangs.

(he pulls a short sword from his cane. He puts himself on guard)

JEAN TAUREAU

Ah! You have a weapon. I didn't expect that!

(He gets ready to jump on Jean Robert where one hears a shivering in the crowd. A young man, dressed as an errand-boy, but with every elegance of costume enters, breaks through the crowd and seizes the compass from Jean Taureau.)

JEAN TAUREAU

(turning) Oh,—traitor!

(stupefied, recognizing the young man) Mr. Salvator!

CROWD

Mr. Salvator!

(The Turk raises his head, opens an eye, then immediately goes back to sleep.)

PÉTRUS

There's a fellow whose name augurs well. Let's see if he will do honor to his name.

SALVATOR

(to Jean Taureau) You are always drunk and quarrelsome?

JEAN TAUREAU

Mr. Salvator, let me explain.

SALVATOR

You are wrong.

JEAN TAUREAU

But let me tell you—

SALVATOR

You are wrong.

JEAN TAUREAU

But still—

SALVATOR

You are wrong, I tell you.

JEAN TAUREAU

But how do you know that since you weren't here?

SALVATOR

Do I need to be here to understand how things happen?

JEAN TAUREAU

It seems to me—still—

SALVATOR

(pointing to the three young men) Look!

JEAN TAUREAU

Well, I'm looking, so?

SALVATOR

What do you see?

JEAN TAUREAU

I see three fops to whom I promised to give a thrashing and who are going to get it, one day or another.

SALVATOR

You see three young men, elegant, well-dressed, who are wrong to come to a dive; but it's no reason to quarrel with them.

JEAN TAUREAU

Me—try to pick a quarrel? I'm incapable of it, Mr. Salvator.

SALVATOR

Look! You are not going to say that they are the ones who provoked you, you and your companions!

JEAN TAUREAU

But still, you can see very plainly that they were in a state of defending themselves.

SALVATOR

Because right was on their side. You think strength is everything, you who changed your name from Barthelmy Lelong to Jean Taureau. You have just had proof to the contrary, God let the lesson profit you.

JEAN TAUREAU

But since I tell you that it was they who called us clowns, rednecks, brutes—

SALVATOR

And why did they call you that?

JEAN TAUREAU

They said we were drunk.

SALVATOR

I ask you why they said that?

JEAN TAUREAU

For nothing, that's why.

SALVATOR

Come on?

JEAN TAUREAU

Because I wanted to make them close the window—

SALVATOR

And you wanted them to close the window because?

JEAN TAUREAU

Because—because I don't like drafts.

SALVATOR

Because you were drunk, as these gentlemen told you, because you wanted to start a dispute with someone and you seized the occasion by its hair, because you had some quarrel at home and you wished to make these innocents pay for the caprices and infidelities of Miss Fifine.

JEAN TAUREAU

Be quiet, Mr. Salvator! Don't pronounce that name. The wretch; she's killing me.

SALVATOR

Ah! You see plainly that I have touched you where it hurts. These gentlemen did well to open the window, the air in here is infected, and as there isn't enough with two open windows, you are going to open the second this instant.

JEAN TAUREAU

Me, go open a window when I asked someone to close the other—me, Barthelmy Lelong—my father's son.

SALVATOR

Yes, you Barthelmy Lelong, drunken brawler, you dishonor the name of your father, and you did well to take another name! I tell you, you are going to open this window as punishment for having insulted these gentlemen.

JEAN TAUREAU

Thunder could explode around my head and I would not obey you.

SALVATOR

Then, I don't know you under any name, you are only a worker— huge and insulting, and I will kick you out from wherever I happen to be. Leave! Well—did you hear me?

JEAN TAUREAU

Yes, but I am not going to go.

SALVATOR

In the name of your father, whose name you invoked just now, I order you to go away.

(He walks toward him.)

JEAN TAUREAU

Mr. Salvator, Mr. Salvator—don't come near me!

SALVATOR

(stamping his foot) You are going to leave!

JEAN TAUREAU

You know very well that you can make me do whatever you wish and that I would cut my hand off rather than strike you. So—you see—

(recoiling, leaving) I leave—

(by the stairs) Oh—but if I ever meet them, they will pay me.

TOUSSAINT

Mr. Salvator, your very humble servant.

(He leaves.)

SAC A PLATRE

Mr. Salvator, I have indeed the honor—you have orders to give me?

SALVATOR

(grabbing his arms) Indeed! You are the least drunk of all.

SAC A PLATRE

You think so?

SALVATOR

You are going to stay at the door and if you see a man dressed like a magician who looks like he's going to enter the cabaret, you will say to him, "Mount Saint John." He will know what that means and go. If he needs you, you will put yourself at his orders.

SAC A PLATRE

Yes, Mr. Salvator.

SALVATOR

To prove that you have my commission, you will imitate the rooster's crowing which you imitate so well, when you go to place a flag on a house.

SAC A PLATRE

As you say, Mr. Salvator. Au revoir, Mr. Salvator.

SALVATOR

Au revoir—and don't let me hear it said that you are mixed up in such a mess. Go!

(During this exchange, the Turk has raised his head but was unable to hear. At the moment Salvator returns, he lets his head fall on the table.)

JEAN ROBERT

(extending his hand to Salvator) Thanks, sir, for delivering us from that drunken fiend.

SALVATOR

It was nothing to speak of, only if you will allow me to give you some advice from a friend? Never put your foot in here again, Mr. Jean Robert.

JEAN ROBERT

You know me, Mr. Salvator?

SALVATOR

As everyone does. Aren't you one of our celebrated poets?

(turning to the crowd) And now folks, you should be content. You've seen something for your money, right? Do me then the courtesy of moving on. There's not air enough in here for four men to breathe. Which means, my good friends, that I wish to be alone with these gentlemen.

(the crowd leaves shouting—"Long live Mr. Salvator"—raising their caps)

(Salvator to the Turk, who is sleeping on the table) And you too—sir, like the others.

(The Turk replies with loud snores.)

JEAN ROBERT

Oh, my word, Mr. Salvator, that one there's sleeping so majestically one hasn't the conscience to wake him.

SALVATOR

(to himself) Yes, perhaps it would be better for him to remain here than others. So, he doesn't irritate you, Mr. Jean Robert?

JEAN ROBERT

Not the least in the world.

SALVATOR

Nor you, Mr. Pétrus?

PÉTRUS

Ah! Ah! You know me, too?

SALVATOR

Nor you, Mr. Ludovic? But what are you looking at?

LUDOVIC

I am looking to see if you haven't one leg shorter than the other.

SALVATOR

Yes, because, in that case, you would greet me by the name of Asmodeus. Tell me, why is it so astonishing that I know a painter who last year had a very nice exhibition, and a young doctor who three months ago passed his examinations with flying colors?

JEAN ROBERT

But you, sir, who know everyone and who appear to be known by everyone, would it be indiscreet to ask you who you are?

SALVATOR

Me, sir? You have heard my name: Salvator. As for my position, I am an errand-boy in the corner of the Rue aux Fers. If you need a sure person to carry your letter and a solid fellow to carry your trunks, I ask your business.

LUDOVIC

What, sir, this costume is not a disguise?

SALVATOR

Not the least in the world. Rather ask the waiter who brought your supper?

WAITER

(with the supper looking at the Turk) What? I thought it was a polichinelle—it's a Turk. I am always making mistakes.

SALVATOR

What's wrong with you, and why don't you serve these gentlemen?

WAITER

Here, gentlemen, here it is. The cutlets are a bit dry and the omelette is a little thick but it's not the fault of the cook.

PÉTRUS

Mr. Salvator, would you do us the honor of supping with us?

SALVATOR

Thanks, gentlemen, but I am going to ask your permission to retire.

PÉTRUS

No manners!

SALVATOR

I am very cognizant of the honor that you are doing me, gentlemen, but it's impossible to accept.

(the young people bow—Salvator, low to the waiter) You don't have some corner from which I won't lose sight of the Turk?

WAITER

On the landing to the right. There's a door which gives on a room. It is empty, you can see from there everything you wish to see.

SALVATOR

That's fine.

(to the young men) Gentlemen!

MR. JACKAL

(aside, raising his head) He's pretending to go, but he's not going. Good! He's in the closet. The curtain has risen.

(He snores.)

WAITER

Do you gentlemen still wish to hear the gypsy sing? According to your orders, gentlemen, she's waiting below with her honorable mother La Brocanti, the most celebrated card-reader of the Faubourg St. Germain, who will do big or small readings for you, and her young brother, Babolin, boy of high hopes, who executes the three postures of body, swallows swords and eats flaming torches.

PÉTRUS

Yes, it's true, and I was forgetting my painting of Mignon! Indeed I should say we are still asking for her; and more than ever.

WAITER

(calling) Eh! La Brocanti, they are asking for you here.

LA BROCANTI

(from below) We'll be there.

(Babolin enters with a series of capers and flips.)

BABOLIN

Hop!

ROSE NOEL

(entering after him) Oh! I thought Mr. Salvator was here.

PÉTRUS

Oh, the charming child! But look, gentlemen!

JEAN ROBERT

(at the sight of La Brocanti) Oh—the horrid witch—don't look, gentlemen.

LA BROCANTI

What do these gentlemen want? Do they want to know the past, the present, or the future? They have inheritances awaiting them. Will they have a good marriage? Will they have a lot of children? Three francs for the big readings and thirty sous for the small ones.

LUDOVIC

Thanks, old lady. We have forgotten the past, we thank God for the present and consequently we are in no hurry about the future. We love our relatives to the twenty-fifth degree and consequently, in no hurry to inherit from them. No, Brocanti, my love, what we wish to see and hear is this charming child.

LA BROCANTI

What do you want her to sing? The complaint of Montebelolo. Brave Frenchmen, spill your tears.

LUDOVIC

Thanks, they sang that when I was in my cradle.

JEAN ROBERT

Can we speak to Rose Noel?

LA BROCANTI

Without doubt.

PÉTRUS

Disturb her the least possible. I am devouring her. She's my Mignon.

BABOLIN

Do you hear, Rose Noel?—he's eating you!

(looking at Pétrus' notebook) Ah, that's what she is all the same!

JEAN ROBERT

Listen, my pretty child.

ROSE NOEL

I am listening, sir.

JEAN ROBERT

Do you not know some gypsy song—something original and poetic?

ROSE NOEL

In German, English or French?

JEAN ROBERT

What, my child, you speak three languages?

LA BROCANTI

God be thanked! Nothing was neglected for her education.

BABOLIN

Oh—what a mother—how expensive that was for her, her education, it's like mine. Say, Rose Noel, La Brocanti is speaking of the education that she gave us, if that doesn't make you shhivverr!

ROSE NOEL

Would you like to hear Marguerite's song from Faust?

BABOLIN

Or the Queen Mab from Shakespeare?

JEAN ROBERT

You know the Queen Mab?

ROSE NOEL

Yes—Mr. Salvator translated it for me.

JEAN ROBERT

What—he's a poet, our errand-boy?

ROSE NOEL

He does what he pleases.

LUDOVIC

Is this some disguised Prince?

PÉTRUS

Imbecile! He cannot compose verse.

JEAN ROBERT

Queen Mab. I wouldn't mind hearing verse by the errand-boy.

BABOLIN

Go for it.

LUDOVIC

Queen Mab! Queen Mab!

JEAN ROBERT

What is this Queen Mab!

ROSE NOEL

(recites)

She is the fairies' midwife, and she comes
In shape no bigger than an agate-stone
On the fore-finger of an alderman,
Drawn with a team of little atomies
Athwart men's noses as they lie asleep;
Her wagon-spokes made of long spiders' legs,
The cover of the wings of grasshoppers,
The traces of the smallest spider's web,
The collars of the moonshine's watery beams,
Her whip of cricket's bone, the lash of film,
Her wagoner a small grey-coated gnat,
Not so big as a round little worm
Prick'd from the lazy finger of a maid;
Her chariot is an empty hazel-nut
Made by the joiner squirrel or old grub,
Time out o' mind the fairies' coachmakers.

And in this state she gallops night by night
Through lovers' brains, and then they dream of love;
O'er courtiers' knees, that dream on court'sies straight,
O'er lawyers' fingers, who straight dream on fees,
O'er ladies' lips, who straight on kisses dream,
Which oft the angry Mab with blisters plagues,
Because their breaths with sweetmeats tainted are:
Sometime she gallops o'er a courtier's nose,
And then dreams he of smelling out a suit;
And sometime comes she with a tithe-pig's tail
Tickling a parson's nose as a' lies asleep,
Then dreams, he of another benefice:
Sometime she driveth o'er a soldier's neck,
And then dreams he of cutting foreign throats,
Of breaches, ambuscadoes, Spanish blades,
Of healths five-fathom deep; and then anon
Drums in his ear, at which he starts and wakes,
And being thus frighted swears a prayer or two
And sleeps again.

ALL

Bravo! Bravo!

JEAN ROBERT

But this Mr. Salvator is a poet, gentlemen.

(takes a saucer for a collection, it produces three coins) Here, my child, this is for you.

BABOLIN

Three gold coins! Say, mom, it's better than the big reading.

PÉTRUS

Where do you live, Brocanti?

LA BROCANTI

Rue Triperti #8, my good sir.

PÉTRUS

That's fine. That's all I wanted to know.

LUDOVIC

What will you do at Brocanti's?

PÉTRUS

I will play the grand game.

LUDOVIC

And now, Brocanti, I have some advice to give you, as a doctor: go home and let this child sleep—and take care of her—she isn't in good health, your child!

BABOLIN

Do you hear, Brocanti? This the same story which Mr. Salvator repeats to you ceaselessly.

LA BROCANTI

Fine, we'll watch over her. Come, little loves.

JEAN ROBERT

Waiter, the bill.

(Rose Noel, Babolin, and La Brocanti leave.)

ROSE NOEL

(to waiter as she leaves) You haven't seen Mr. Salvator?

WAITER

No, Miss Rose Noel—no.

JEAN ROBERT

The bill.

WAITER

Here.

JEAN ROBERT

Thirty-five francs for six dozen oysters, six cutlets, an omelette and three bottles of Chablis?

WAITER

And—a broken table and two broken chairs.

JEAN ROBERT

That's fair. Here's forty. The rest is a tip.

PÉTRUS

Well, are you happy with your night, Jean Robert?

JEAN ROBERT

Admit there was a moment where you would have preferred to be at the Rock than here?

LUDOVIC

My word, I confess it, and you Pétrus?

PÉTRUS

No, there I would not have met Rose Noel, and thanks to Rose Noel, my picture of Mignon is finished.

JEAN ROBERT

You are going to put her in it?

PÉTRUS

As of tomorrow.

LUDOVIC

And the portrait of Miss de Valgeneuse?

PÉTRUS

The two things go together. One is work, the other is art.

JEAN ROBERT

And when can we see the rough draft?

PÉTRUS

In three days, at two in the afternoon at my workshop, Rue de l'Ouest.

LUDOVIC

(pointing to the Turk) Should we do this brave man the service of waking him before we leave?

JEAN ROBERT

For what? He dreams he's in Mohammed's paradise. Let him dream—the hours are rare.

(They hear the rooster crowing.)

PÉTRUS

My goodness—it's the cock singing.

JEAN ROBERT

Which proves it is two in the morning.

(They leave.)

SALVATOR

(enters and goes to Mr. Jackal) Now, Mr. Jackal, you can wake up, take off your false nose, put on your glasses and have some tobacco. The one who was waiting for you will no longer do so.

(Mr. Jackal raises his head, puts on his spectacles, takes out some tobacco and offers some to Salvator.)

MR. JACKAL

Do you use this, Mr. Salvator?

SALVATOR

Never.

MR. JACKAL

Let's go. I'm done up.

SALVATOR

Console yourself—only strong men can admit things like that.

MR. JACKAL

Because they hope to take their revenge.

SALVATOR

(ready to leave) After you—honor to those who deserve it.

CURTAIN

ACT I

SCENE 3

Pétrus' workshop. Very elegant with trophies, armor, pictures, etc.

Suzanne poses on a couch. Loredan is amusing himself with a flower. Jean Robert is seated writing some verse in a notebook.

PÉTRUS

It is with the most profound regret, Miss, that I must tell you our sitting will be curtailed today.

SUZANNE

And why will our sitting be curtailed today—if you please, Master Van Dyck?

PÉTRUS

Because I was expecting you yesterday and not today.

SUZANNE

What do you want? Yesterday I couldn't come. Ah, you think that the pensioners of Madame Adrienne Desmarest are free like the students of Mr. Gros or Mr. Horace Vernet? No, know this, what fame ought to have taught you: it was Madame's party yesterday like they said at Vanvres, and we were ordered to be gay under pain of punishment. They dined in families with three extras—cabbage in the soup, parsley around the beef, and eggs in the salad. They drank her health with some wine d'Argenteuil, and then for dessert, she was taken on foot to stroll with Diogenes' lantern—with permission to pick the daisies but forbidden to strip the leaves from them to tell fortunes. We were very amused—go!

PÉTRUS

You would be much more amused here?

SUZANNE

Indeed, I think so. First of all, I find you charming.

PÉTRUS

(to Loredan)

You hear, sir. Your sister has made me a declaration.

LOREDAN

Let her do it and don't believe a word she says; Suzanne is the greatest coquette I know.

SUZANNE

But at least wait until I tell you why I find you charming.

PÉTRUS

Oh—there's a reason.

SUZANNE

Right! You think it's because you call yourself Pierre de Courtney; you think it's because your uncle the Marquis de Herbel lets you have fifty thousand pounds; you think it's because you are dressed by the best tailor in Paris—that I find you charming? No—it's because you let me stay still while I'm posing, it's because your friend, Mr. Ludovic gives me powder for my teeth and rouge for my lips. It's even because Mr. Jean Robert is of an agreeable conversation, when he isn't composing verse—Mr. Jean Robert!

JEAN ROBERT

Miss?

SUZANNE

For whom, please, are you composing verse?

JEAN ROBERT

For a gypsy girl, miss.

SUZANNE

What! you know a gypsy girl?

JEAN ROBERT

A dramatic author has to know everybody.

SUZANNE

My dear brother, Loredan, do me the favor of reading over Mr. Jean Robert's shoulder the verse he's composing, and if they can be repeated to a girl like me, tell them to me.

PÉTRUS

Would you be good enough to turn a little more to the right, Miss? I want to see your left eye.

SUZANNE

Don't forget my wink; it's the best thing I've got in my face.

PÉTRUS

You make a good bargain with the rest!

LOREDAN

Mr. Jean Robert's verses are charming.

JEAN ROBERT

Only you know they are not mine.

SUZANNE

And whose are they?

JEAN ROBERT

Goethe's. Do you know the novel, *Wilhelm Meister*?

SUZANNE

A young woman named Miss de Valgeneuse and who is Madame Desmarest's pension, does not read novels, sir, and is unfamiliar with *Wilhelm Meister*. By chance, are you translating the song of Mignon?

JEAN ROBERT

Exactly. But if you don't know the novel how do you know the song?

SUZANNE

Who doesn't know the song "Kennst du das Land?" Read your translation, Mr. Jean Robert, so I can see if it is exact.

JEAN ROBERT

I would like nothing better, but the last four verses are not finished.

SUZANNE

Finish your last four verses and during that time, Mr. Pétrus will explain to me why he cannot accord me a full sitting today.

PÉTRUS

Because I am waiting for this same gypsy for whom Jean Robert is writing verses.

SUZANNE

A true gypsy?

PÉTRUS

Oh, as to that, there's no way to be sure, is there?

SUZANNE

It seems there's a novel here; and ought one to take an interest in it?

PÉTRUS

For us, until today, the story or rather, what we know if it, is very simple.

SUZANNE

May I hear it?

PÉTRUS

Of course.

SUZANNE

Speak, I am listening. What a misfortune that Mr. Jean Robert hasn't finished his song. He would have made this simple story into a very complicated drama.

JEAN ROBERT

Help me to rhyme "beloved," Pétrus, I am stupid today.

SUZANNE

"Charmed."

JEAN ROBERT

Thanks, Miss.

PÉTRUS

You see, you must be satisfied with my narrative.

SUZANNE

Did you notice that if King Louis XIV failed to wait, I, I am waiting.

PÉTRUS

Imagine then that Tuesday in the midst of the Ball at the Opera, the idea came to us—to Ludovic, Jean Robert and myself—the stupid idea of having supper in a cabaret at la Halle.

SUZANNE

What are you saying?

PÉTRUS

In a cabaret.

SUZANNE

In la Halle?

PÉTRUS

In la Halle.

SUZANNE

I compliment you on that.

LOREDAN

It was very well done in the time of the Regency.

SUZANNE

Yes, but in the year 1827 under His Majesty Charles X?

LOREDAN

I wish I had known; I'd have gone with you.

SUZANNE

Fie! And in this cabaret?

PÉTRUS

From the opinion that you are manifesting, I don't know if I should continue.

SUZANNE

Keep talking! This interests me a great deal. Only, I find there are delays in your story.

PÉTRUS

I am hastening to the denouement. In this cabaret we met a ravishing little gypsy.

SUZANNE

Gypsies are always ravishing to painters. It's only women of the world who are ugly.

PÉTRUS

You cannot say that of me, Miss, since I've tried to paint your portrait. I cannot complain of anything except that you are too pretty!

SUZANNE

Should I get up and curtsy to you?

PÉTRUS

One doesn't curtsy except to liars.

SUZANNE

Well, you met a ravishing little gypsy?

PÉTRUS

Who sang, who dances, who recited poetry—the true type of Mignon.

SUZANNE

And when she turned her head toward you, you decided to do a painting?

PÉTRUS

Right-o!

SUZANNE

And she's the one who's coming today?

PÉTRUS

It's she.

SUZANNE

So that it's simply this little vagabond who's shortening my sitting?

PÉTRUS

The poor child will earn a crown, more perhaps than she could earn in a month.

SUZANNE

And she's coming all alone like that, to find her money?

PÉTRUS

Not at all, on the contrary! She's tied to the skirts of her mother, a horrible witch named la Brocanti, who reads cards—not to mention her brother, who's nourishing the ambition to become a clown.

SUZANNE

Well, while you are painting the daughter, I will have my fortune told by the mother.

LOREDAN

That's an idea!

PÉTRUS

Well, but what will Madame Desmarest say?

SUZANNE

She's not here—I am under the protection of my brother.

LOREDAN

And I permit the fortunetelling.

(A knock on the door.)

SUZANNE

Is that your gypsy?

PÉTRUS

I don't believe so. That's Ludovic's knock. Can he come in?

SUZANNE

I know him well. Enter!

LOREDAN

(entering and going to Suzanne) Miss, although I never hoped to meet you here, I am going to prove that I executed your orders. Here's the powder for your teeth and the rouge for your lips.

SUZANNE

Mr. Ludovic, I promise to be your client as soon as I am better.

LOREDAN

Have you fallen ill?

SUZANNE

The conventions require that I go to an old doctor of seventy, who will kill me. The same conventions don't permit a doctor of twenty-five to treat a sick girl of nineteen.

LUDOVIC

Fine! You must outrage the conventions and get better!

(to Pétrus) My dear Pétrus, I have just looked a long way off and I just heard a carriage stop at your door, which seemed to me to have the honor of conveying Miss Rose Noel and her respectable family.

SUZANNE

She's called Rose Noel?

PÉTRUS

Yes, don't you find the name pretty?

SUZANNE

Indeed.

PÉTRUS

It is indeed them. I hear them coming up. Excuse me, Miss.

SUZANNE

I hope you aren't going to deprive us of this ravishing person?

PÉTRUS

On the contrary, I am going to put her in a costume of my choice which is waiting in a neighboring room—and I am going to present her to you in all her splendor.

(Pétrus goes out.)

SUZANNE

Well, are those verses ready, Mr. Jean Robert?

JEAN ROBERT

Alas, yes, miss.

SUZANNE

Why "alas"?

JEAN ROBERT

Because they are not good.

LOREDAN

Shut up! They are charming.

LUDOVIC

Which of these two to believe?

SUZANNE

Give them here. I promise you a judgment whose impartiality will rival that of Solomon.

LUDOVIC

Let us hear.

JEAN ROBERT

You know—it's Mignon's song.

SUZANNE

We know.

(reading)

Do you know the land where the orange blossoms bloom,
Where the orange ripens under its green leaves
Where the days are burning and the nights are tepid,
Where Spring reigns, and exiles Winter?
This sweet land where the solitary myrtle thrives
Where the laurel grows in a perfumed air.
Tell me, do you know where it is? No? Know, well it's the earth
That I want to return to with you, beloved!

Do you know the house where my eye opens
Where those gods of granite who terrify me,
As they see me return, with their stony lips
Murmuring: "Child, what have they done to you?"

Each night, like a beacon, in my dream shining
It's pain which ignites the enflamed sleeper.
Tell me, do you know that house? It's the one

Where I would have wanted to live with you, beloved!

(Rose Noel in Mignon's costume enters by the side door, pushed by Pétrus then stops without Suzanne seeing her. Babolin and La Brocanti enter as well.)

(Suzanne continues to recite)

Do you know the mountain where the avalanche glitters
Where the mule travels along a misty footpath
Where an old dragon crouches with its brood,
Where the foaming torrent leaps on the rocks?
That mountain must cross it in the clouds,
It's from its summit that the charmed gaze
Discovers on the horizon the familiar land
Where I want to die with you, beloved.

ROSE NOEL

Oh! It's Mignon. It's Mignon's song. Oh—Miss, for the love of God, give it to me—I have heard it sung in German, when I was little and I've never been able to find it since.

(Suzanne gives it to her.)

PÉTRUS

Now, my sweet Rose Noel, will you come pose as Mignon?

ROSE NOEL

For Mignon. I want to.

(Pétrus puts her in an agreeable position.)

BABOLIN

Ah, I wish they'd paint my picture, too.

LA BROCANTI

Mr. Babolin, the society in which we find ourselves is not that in which we are accustomed to travel, so you are going to do me the pleasure of waiting for me outside.

BABOLIN

But if Rose Noel can stay in your society, why can't I?

LA BROCANTI

Because Rose Noel is an artist.

BABOLIN

I am not an artist. Well, that's new!

(He leaves, grumbling)

LOREDAN

(to his sister)

Do you know this child is truly charming?

SUZANNE

You're not going to become amorous, too?

LOREDAN

Why not?

SUZANNE

Say, Madame Brocanti! That's your name isn't it?

LA BROCANTI

To serve you, my pretty miss.

SUZANNE

They assure me you tell fortunes.

LA BROCANTI

That's my business.

SUZANNE

And in what manner do you do it?

LA BROCANTI

In every way: with cards, with coffee stains; in your hand—and infallibly. Mrs. Lenormand was my aunt, you know who predicted to Madame de Beauharnais.

LOREDAN

That she would marry Bonaparte and become Empress?

PÉTRUS

(satisfied with Rose Noel's pose) She's charming like that, isn't she Jean Robert?

JEAN ROBERT

Charming!

SUZANNE

(drawing off her glove) Here's my hand, good woman.

LUDOVIC

(to Suzanne) May we listen?

SUZANNE

Yes, for those who, like me, want to waste their time.

LA BROCANTI

What do you want to know; the past, the present, or the future?

LUDOVIC

You see, you have choices.

SUZANNE

What do you advise me?

LUDOVIC

The future. At your age you don't have a past.

SUZANNE

That's what you think! I have one and I wish to be told about it. Let's hear about my past.

LA BROCANTI

Here—aristocratic hand, long, fine, without connection to the phalanges, straight nails, hand of a duchess; idle but prodigious hand.

SUZANNE

Ought I to take all that as so many compliments?

LA BROCANTI

I though you asked for the truth?

SUZANNE

Continue.

LA BROCANTI

You are rich! Very rich.

SUZANNE

What news! You saw my coachman and carriage at the door.

LA BROCANTI

Although rich, you are ambitious for fortune, although noble, you are ambitious of honors.

SUZANNE

Eh—well, that is true enough.

LUDOVIC

You admit ambition.

SUZANNE

Oh—I am very frank.

LA BROCANTI

You have, in the last eighteen months lost a close relative.

SUZANNE

That's true enough.

(pointing to her brother) Then I suppose I'll marry this gentleman?

LA BROCANTI

(to Loredan) Give me your hand, if you please, young man.

(she takes a magnifying glass from her pocket and looks at his hand with it) Similar hand—family line. You try to deceive me, Miss. This gentlemen is not your husband. He is near relative—probably your brother.

LOREDAN

What do you say to that Suzanne?

LUDOVIC

This is becoming very interesting, it seems to me.

SUZANNE

For that reason, I give you your liberty, gentlemen.

LUDOVIC

You kick us out—?

SUZANNE

Just a bit farther off.

(Ludovic bows and separates himself.)

LOREDAN

By chance, is this La Brocanti a real witch?

LA BROCANTI

Must I say all that I see in your hand?

SUZANNE

All.

LA BROCANTI

But suppose you get angry?

SUZANNE

I won't get angry.

LA BROCANTI

I told you that, although rich, you were ambitious of fortune, that, although noble you were ambitious of honors, and I am going to add although young and pretty, you have never loved, and probably—

SUZANNE

Probably?

LA BROCANTI

You will never love.

SUZANNE

Where do you see that?

LA BROCANTI

The line of the heart is barely indicated—and that of the head cuts the line in two.

LOREDAN

(laughing) Go on, go on, Mother. You are in the right.

SUZANNE

(to Loredan) Wait.

(to Brocanti) But suppose I have never loved because I've never been loved.

LA BROCANTI

You have been loved—and a lot. You have been loved too much!

SUZANNE

Is anyone ever loved too much?

LA BROCANTI

Do you want to turn to the present?

LOREDAN

Not at all. The past is very interesting. I knew nothing of all this. I was on a trip with my tutor and I stayed away five years. Well, my sister proves the maxim: "Men keep others' secrets best, but women keep their own best."

LA BROCANTI

I would prefer not to continue my pretty miss.

SUZANNE

And why is that?

LA BROCANTI

Science cannot be mistaken and sometimes it says things that are displeasing.

SUZANNE

There, let's finish! I have been loved too much—and what as the result of this love?

LA BROCANTI

A great misfortune!

(brother and sister look at each other) A death, here's a star beside the life line.

SUZANNE

Well, what does this star say?

LA BROCANTI

I cannot be mistaken, Miss. Think it over carefully.

LOREDAN

My sister is asking you what this star means.

LA BROCANTI

What it means—

SUZANNE

Speak, will you!

LA BROCANTI

Very well, since you absolutely insist, Miss—it means that someone who loved you killed himself for you!

SUZANNE

(rising) Enough!

LOREDAN

What are you talking about?

SUZANNE

I say this woman is probably from the police. Give her a crown, and let her go.

LA BROCANTI

Saving your respect, Miss, I cannot go until Mr. Pétrus has finished with little Rose Noel.

SUZANNE

(giving her a crown) Here!

LOREDAN

(low to Suzanne) Could she be speaking of our cousin Conrad?

SUZANNE

I don't know who she means.

(She goes to the window and leans her face against it.)

BABOLIN

(popping his head in the door) Pardon everyone! Which one of these gentlemen is called Jean Robert?

JEAN ROBERT

I am.

BABOLIN

The errand-boy from the Rue aux Fers has a letter for you.

JEAN ROBERT

Salvator?

BABOLIN

Yes.

ALL

Salvator.

ROSE NOEL

(joyously) Salvator.

JEAN ROBERT

(to Suzanne) Miss, you were asking me for a novel just now. I have better than a novel to offer you. I have an enigma. An errand-boy who—day before yesterday, in the cabaret Pétrus was telling you of, saved our lives, who has the manners of a gentleman and who writes verse like Lamartine. Would you have him come in?

SUZANNE

Willingly. I love enigmas when I don't have to solve them.

PÉTRUS

(without leaving his palette and his brush) Dear Mr. Salvator, do us the pleasure of entering!

SALVATOR

(entering) Mr. Jean Robert, I have only a letter to bring to you; but I was urged to bring it myself. The lady will look for her reply at your place at five o'clock this evening, Rue de l'University. Now that my commission is performed, and the postage paid—

SUZANNE

This is strange. That voice.

PÉTRUS

But no, no, no. We won't let you go so easily. Come in. Come in.

LOREDAN

(in a low voice)

Much ceremony for an errand-boy.

SUZANNE

(aside, seeing Salvator) Conrad!

SALVATOR

Suzanne!

ROSE NOEL

Good day, Mr. Salvator.

SALVATOR

Good day, my child.

JEAN ROBERT

You don't know who this letter is from?

SALVATOR

It doesn't contain anything irritating, I hope?

JEAN ROBERT

No.

(to Ludovic) It is from that poor Dominican monk who was in pension with us.

LUDOVIC

Dominique?

PÉTRUS

Dominique! The one whose father was involved in that strange and terrible affair! What was his family name?

LUDOVIC

What—wait—

JEAN ROBERT

Sarranti, by God.

ROSE NOEL

Sarranti.

SALVATOR

What's wrong with you?

ROSE NOEL

Nothing. Nothing's wrong with me!

LUDOVIC

And he writes you?

JEAN ROBERT

To tell me that he will be at my house today at five o'clock.

SALVATOR

As he wrote, "Rush" on the letter and I knew you were here, I came.

JEAN ROBERT

He says he needs all my friendship.

LOREDAN

(searing in his turn) Sarranti! Sarranti! I have heard that name.

A Bonapartist who was accused of having stolen a hundred thousand crowns and murdering two children—the nephews of a certain Mr. Gérard.

ROSE NOEL

(putting her hand to her heart) Ah!

LOREDAN

The affair made enough noise, so that it is easy to remember.

SUZANNE

Mr. Gérard. I knew him. A saintly man who contributes to the Prix Montoyon.

ROSE NOEL

(interrupting) Mr. Pétrus, if you would permit me.

PÉTRUS

What's wrong, Miss?

LA BROCANTI

What's wrong?

ROSE NOEL

I don't know if this setting is tiring me, but—

PÉTRUS

Brocanti, take your child to the room where she changed. You will find water, sugar and orangeade.

ROSE NOEL

(prayerfully) Don't go, Mr. Salvator.

SALVATOR

No, be tranquil, my child.

BABOLIN

(stupefied) Ah, Rose Noel feels ill!

(sitting in the armchair she vacated) As for me I don't feel too
bad—On the contrary.

(Rose Noel leaves with Brocanti.)

SALVATOR

Did you notice that this child repeated the name of Mr. Sarranti?

JEAN ROBERT

Yes.

SALVATOR

That she went pale at that of Mr. Gérard?

LUDOVIC

Yes.

LOREDAN

But you who are, or appear to be, her confidant, if the thing upsets you, she will tell you.

SALVATOR

(dreamily) Perhaps.

BABOLIN

Say, Mr. Pétrus, there's a scratching at your door.

LUDOVIC

Exactly like the King's.

BABOLIN

(opening the door) Oh—a dog who is big as the elephant at the Bastille.

(Shuts the door.)

SALVATOR

It's Roland who followed me. I left him in the street but when someone came in, he slid in.

PÉTRUS

Babolin, I name you introducer of Ambassadors—let Roland enter. Who loves the master, loves the dog.

BABOLIN

(announcing) Mr. Roland.

JEAN ROBERT

Oh—the beautiful beast.

SALVATOR

You can indeed say "oh, the fine beast." Go say good day to these gentlemen, Roland.

LUDOVIC

(feeling the sides of the dog) Really, he's received a nasty wound, your dog, Mr. Salvator—and I don't know a Christian who wouldn't return it.

(to dog) You were at war, my boy.

SALVATOR

It seems.

PÉTRUS

What do you mean "it seems."

SALVATOR

On that point I know no more than you, gentlemen. I hunted for five or six years in the environs of Paris.

LOREDAN

(with surprise) You hunted?

SALVATOR

I mean I was poaching; an errand-boy doesn't hunt. I found this poor animal all bloody, dying in a ditch. His beauty and his suffering excited my compassion. I took him to a fountain. I washed him with fresh water. He appeared reborn from the care I took of him—that night I treated his wounds—and cured by me, Roland has vowed me recognition which would shame a man—right Roland?

(Roland comes to rub against Salvator and puts his two paws on his breast. The door of the room opens. Rose Noel and Brocanti enter.)

SUZANNE

Ah—here's the lady of the vapors—who's getting better so it seems.

SALVATOR

What's wrong with you, Roland?

LA BROCANTI

What's wrong with you, Rose Noel?

ROSE NOEL

(suffocating with joy) Oh—my good dog—is it you?

(Roland escapes from Salvator and rushes to Rose Noel.)

ALL

Roland! Roland!

(They try to stop Roland.)

ROSE NOEL

Oh, gentleman, don't harm Brésil.

SALVATOR

You know Roland!

ROSE NOEL

He's not called Roland. He's called Brésil.

SALVATOR

And where did you know Brésil? Tell me that.

ROSE NOEL

Where did I know Brésil?

SALVATOR

Yes—can you tell me that?

ROSE NOEL

(frightened) No, no, no! Impossible! My brother! My poor brother! Oh, Madame Orsola—Madame Orsola! Don't kill me!

ALL

Madame Orsola?

(Rose Noel faints. They group around her.)

CURTAIN

ACT II
SCENE 4

La Brocanti's loft. To the right a garret reached by a staircase. Midnight.

La Brocanti, counting some money. Babolin is making a pack of clothes.

LA BROCANTI

Let's see. What are you doing rummaging about, vagabond?

BABOLIN

I am putting my clothes together.

LA BROCANTI

And what for?

BABOLIN

To remove them.

LA BROCANTI

What! You're moving?

BABOLIN

My lease isn't up, I'm well aware, but I'm in a hurry.

LA BROCANTI

You are going away, wretch?

BABOLIN

Ah, fine! You don't believe I am going to stay here when Rose Noel is no longer here. Not in this life.

LA BROCANTI

But, ingrate, weren't you lodged, nourished and clothed?

BABOLIN

Yes, let's talk of that. Lodged in the attic—that means freezing in the winter, roasted in the summer, nourished with cabbage stalks, the shells of peas, and carrot tops. "Waiter, a toothpick for Mr. Babolin so we can go over the bill together." Dressed! When one thinks what my Sunday dress was, it would give me a vivid idea of the old days, huh? What misery! What misery!

LA BROCANTI

So! You abandon me.

BABOLIN

Why not? You are rich. You've sold Rose Noel for two hundred pounds of income for life, and a thousand shillings down—and that on the sole condition you have no rights to her and that Mr. Salvator will be her tutor. Rose Noel is in a grand pension, where she will become a great lady, and which she will leave to marry a millionaire; her future is assured. It is time I thought of mine.

LA BROCANTI

Do you want me to predict your future?

BABOLIN

Known already, mother. I will end in the galleys. I will die on the scaffold. That's it, isn't it?

LA BROCANTI

Yes, that's it!

BABOLIN

Well, let's leave that and without bitterness. Goodbye, Brocanti.

LA BROCANTI

But first what are you taking in that package?

BABOLIN

Aren't you afraid that it's your gold? I'm not taking anything which is not mine! My rug, for making the leap. My candlestick to make a split pear and my wooden bowl to receive the offerings of society. You don't count on making the jump or a split pear, right, Mother? Well, I leave you your establishment, leave me mine.

LA BROCANTI

Go away! I give you my curse!

BABOLIN

Thanks! It's the first time you've given me something.

LA BROCANTI

May the devil break your bones!

BABOLIN

(on the stairs) Phooey! Pay no attention, it's Babolin, who tumbles.

(opening the door) Say, La Brocanti, now you have income, you must put lights on the stairs.

VOICE

(from below) (imitating an English accent) Hola—in the loft! Can you give me a light?

BABOLIN

Ah, an Englishman. La Brocanti receiving an Englishman at midnight. That's going to be funny. I'm not going yet. Come up, Milord.

(Enter Gibassier disguised as an Englishman.)

GIBASSIER

Isn't this the apartment of Madame La Brocanti?

LA BROCANTI

Yes, sir.

BABOLIN

(aside) He must be an Englishman to call this an apartment.

GIBASSIER

Oh—I want cards read for me.

LA BROCANTI

That's easy, Milord. Three francs for a short reading, six for a long.

GIBASSIER

Oh—I thought it was thirty sous for the short and three francs for the long?

BABOLIN

Yes, but for the English, it is double. Please sit down, Milord.

(he sits on his trunk) Tell for him! Tell for him.

GIBASSIER

I will make a sacrifice to have the long reading.

BABOLIN

And Milord is right, you can't bargain with the cards.

GIBASSIER

Milord wants nothing to do with that.

LA BROCANTI

What does Milord wish then?

GIBASSIER

(low and in his natural voice) First, I want you to send that maggot, who irritates me, away.

BABOLIN

(aside) I thought he called me a maggot—oh, if I was sure of it.

(He goes behind Gibassier and threatens him from behind.)

GIBASSIER

Well, my boy!

BABOLIN

It wasn't "maggot"—it was "my boy"—a compliment.

GIBASSIER

(how to La Brocanti) Well, send him off then.

LA BROCANTI

(aside, astonished) I know this voice, I know it.

BABOLIN

(aside) He whispered in her ear. What did he say?

GIBASSIER

It was three days ago, no—four days ago or rather four days when at the Opera ball, they stole a considerable sum from me.

BABOLIN

It wasn't me—I wasn't there. I was at Bordier's in La Halle. I can prove an alibi.

GIBASSIER

(low to La Brocanti) Send this kid away, as I told you.

BABOLIN

(aside) He spoke to her again, very low.

LA BROCANTI

Babolin, you see that door there?

BABOLIN

Certainly, I see it.

LA BROCANTI

Well, you understand when one shows the door to someone, it's so he will leave.

BABOLIN

That's fine! Let's get going. I would already have been on the Rue Rivali if you hadn't kept me.

(aside) They have some secrets together. Oh, he's a fake Englishman. He didn't say "Goddamn" even once.

(aloud) Time to go.

LA BROCANTI

Fine. And let me hear you close the street door.

(Babolin leaves.)

GIBASSIER

While waiting—

(looks to make sure Babolin is not listening at the door) Let's close this. Two precautions are worth more than one.

(he closes the door, then returning to Brocanti) Ah, since you have already recognized my voice, I hope you will recognize my face as well.

LA BROCANTI

Gibassier! I thought you were in the Midi.

GIBASSIER

Indeed, I was there. For the last three days, I've been in Paris. I travel.

LA BROCANTI

And what do you do in Paris?

GIBASSIER

I come to put up with La Brocanti for a night and a day. Tomorrow, at the same hour, I will take leave of you, my pretty hostess, is it agreed?

LA BROCANTI

You know I can refuse you nothing.

GIBASSIER

Yes. I know it. But first and above all, you are going to remember something. It's that I arrived here at ten-thirty precisely.

LA BROCANTI

But midnight just tolled at Saint Sulpice.

GIBASSIER

All the more reason.

LA BROCANTI

I don't understand.

GIBASSIER

You don't need to understand, only if by chance someone wished to ask you, "Woman Catherine Couturier, called La Brocanti, at what time on Sunday the twenty-eighth of February did Jean Chrysostome Gibassier enter your house?" you will reply simply: "At ten-thirty that evening."

LA BROCANTI

Meaning at ten-thirty tonight you did something?

GIBASSIER

Perhaps.

LA BROCANTI

Something bad?

GIBASSIER

It's possible, but I am not uneasy. I know your address, my chicken, and I said to myself, "I have a good friend where they'll never look for me since we've been separated for five years and no one's ever seen me in Paris with her." Without which you understand there's a fellow who frequents the quays: a certain Mr. Jackal, whose motto is "Cherchez la femme." Hush!

LA BROCANTI

What?

GIBASSIER

It seems to me someone is coming up.

LA BROCANTI

I heard nothing.

GIBASSIER

I hear a crack on the stairs.

LA BROCANTI

What do you mean, Jean! I am getting old—

GIBASSIER

Are you trying to make me believe you've never been young—
where can I hide?

LA BROCANTI

In the attic.

GIBASSIER

Is there a way out?

LA BROCANTI

On the roof, through the skylight.

GIBASSIER

The devil! At this time of year, the roofs are slippery. But I can
take off my shoes.

(He hides in the attic. A knock.)

LA BROCANTI

Are you all right up there?

GIBASSIER

Yes. Don't forget, ten-thirty.

LA BROCANTI

Agreed.

(more knocking) Go away. Who can come at this hour?

(she opens the door. Mr. Jackal enters with a cellar light in his hand) (stupefied) Mr. Jackal!

MR. JACKAL

Yes, respectable Brocanti, Mr. Jackal in person, at such an unreasonable hour. But, what do you want? The malefactors give me so much business during the day, that only the night remains for me to consecrate to honest people.

GIBASSIER

Mr. Jackal!

LA BROCANTI

Mr. Jackal at my house. It's such a great honor, I can't believe it.

MR. JACKAL

And that's what troubles you, I suspect.

(he puts on his spectacles, looks at La Brocanti, and takes a step) Didn't you ask yesterday to renew your license as a card-reader?

LA BROCANTI

Yes, Mr. Jackal.

MR. JACKAL

Well, I signed your license and I brought it myself.

GIBASSIER

(aside) That's not natural. Take care, Gibassier.

(He raises the skylight.)

LA BROCANTI

Who's moving around up in the attic?

LA BROCANTI

It's the rats.

LA BROCANTI

You have rats?

LA BROCANTI

A whole lot, Mr. Jackal.

MR. JACKAL

That's astonishing in an apartment so well decorated. But let's leave the rats and return to the sheep. Did you know, oh, seven or eight years ago, about a fourth of a league from Essone a certain Catherine Couturier?

GIBASSIER

(aside) The devil. This is becoming interesting.

LA BROCANTI

Mr. Jackal.

MR. JACKAL

Answer yes or no!

LA BROCANTI

Yes.

MR. JACKAL

You knew her. Fine.

(takes a step) Wasn't she a cook to the used furniture dealers in the Faubourg St. Antoine, retired after two years?

LA BROCANTI

Yes, Mr. Jackal.

MR. JACKAL

Didn't she have a lover?

LA BROCANTI

Oh—Mr. Jackal.

MR. JACKAL

Reply yes or no. Didn't she have a lover—and this lover, wasn't he called Jean-Chrysostome Gibassier?

GIBASSIER

(aside) Wow!

LA BROCANTI

Alas, yes, Mr. Jackal.

MR. JACKAL

There's an "alas" which is a good augur for the future. Let's continue. This lover, didn't he come in the house through the first floor window?

LA BROCANTI

How do you know all that?

MR. JACKAL

The important thing is that I do know it.

GIBASSIER

(aside) Is he informed! Is he informed!

MR. JACKAL

One night—it was a Friday or Saturday, a night when the masters were absent, Catherine, as was her custom, opened the window to her lover, only this time Master Jean-Chrysostome Gibassier was followed by three friends who entered after him, garrotted Catherine, and visited the entire house, reaping from their visit twenty-four gold plates, a dozen sweets, more or less of little coffee spoons and five thousand francs, thirty thousand bills of exchange, the rest in gold or silver. All this—is it correct?

GIBASSIER

(aside) There must have been one among the four who was a chatterbox.

LA BROCANTI

All this is true, Mr. Jackal, but you know I took—you know that I gained nothing from the theft.

MR. JACKAL

Ah—ah—it was you then, Catherine Couturier?

(He raises his spectacles, looks at Brocanti and takes a step.)

LA BROCANTI

Eh! You know very well it was me, but you know also that I am not a thief.

MR. JACKAL

No, but you left with the thieves. Do you remember the date?

LA BROCANTI

It was the night of May 20th, 1820.

MR. JACKAL

Come, I see that you have a good memory! Let's continue. You left around eight at night in a wicker carriage with a fast horse so that towards 11 p.m. you were already near Juvrier. The carriage stopped. The men got out to get provisions.

GIBASSIER

(aside) There's no way to deny it.

MR. JACKAL

While you were alone you saw a little girl of eight or nine running across the fields, pale, frightened, breathless, who threw herself in your arms, crying "Save me, they want to kill me." This little girl was losing blood from a wound she had received under her clavicle.

LA BROCANTI

(pointing with her finger) Here, right here. The scar is still there.

MR. JACKAL

So much the better! You had pity on her, you took her, you hid her in the straw of the carriage?

LA BROCANTI

Did I do wrong, Mr. Jackal?

MR. JACKAL

One never does wrong to perform a good act, Brocanti! And it is that good action which protects you from me.

LA BROCANTI

Oh, Great God, Mr. Jackal, if I have you for a protector, I need fear no one, and all goes well.

MR. JACKAL

I never told you things were going wrong, Brocanti.

LA BROCANTI

Oh—you warm my heart.

GIBASSIER

What the devil is he getting at?

MR. JACKAL

You reached Entretat—you took a fishing boat to Holland, from Holland to Germany, from Germany to Bohemia. It's there your lover abandoned you with little Rose Noel. But as she was inclined to music and dancing, you taught her to sing, dance and play the guitar. For your part, in your relations with the Bohemians, you learned to read cards and tell fortunes, which means living at the expense of imbeciles. Imbeciles have to be good for something. So long as you preferred to remain out of

France, it was no business of mine. But then there came a time you returned to Paris, where you told fortunes and read cards at your home or in town—and whatever happens on the streets of the King is my concern. I need to know for the moment whose daughter Rose Noel is—who gave her the knife wound of which she bears the scar on her neck—and who she was afraid of when she fled Viry sur Orge.

LA BROCANTI

Damn, Mr. Jackal, only Rose Noel can tell you that.

MR. JACKAL

It's to see her that I came to see you. Where is Rose Noel?

LA BROCANTI

Rose Noel is no longer here, Mr. Jackal.

MR. JACKAL

What, she isn't here?

LA BROCANTI

No.

MR. JACKAL

And since when?

LA BROCANTI

Since the day before yesterday.

MR. JACKAL

Brocanti! Brocanti!

LA BROCANTI

Really, I tell you she is not here.

MR. JACKAL

And where is she?

LA BROCANTI

I don't know.

MR. JACKAL

Take care, Brocanti, take care!

LA BROCANTI

My good, Mr. Jackal, I swear that I tell you the truth. God's own truth. Here's how the thing happened. On the night of the Mardi Gras, three young men were supping at Bordier's at La Halle. They asked for Rose Noel.

MR. JACKAL

I know that.

LA BROCANTI

They made her recite verse.

MR. JACKAL

I know that.

LA BROCANTI

And they gave her two crowns.

MR. JACKAL

No, three.

LA BROCANTI

What? Were you there, too?

MR. JACKAL

Continue.

LA BROCANTI

After Rose Noel recited verse, one of the three men—a painter.

MR. JACKAL

Mr. Pétrus.

LA BROCANTI

Yes! He offered me three crowns for a setting if Rose Noel would pose in his studio. I saw no problem and the next day we went there. There were two friends of Mr. Pétrus and another gentleman with his sister. Mr. Salvator came bringing a letter to Mr. Jean Robert. He came with his dog. Rose Noel was afraid of the dog and fainted. I don't know what took place between these gentlemen and this lady, who are united in a spirit of friendship. Anyway, when Rose Noel came to her senses, they told me Rose Noel couldn't stay with me anymore, that she was too weak to do the job I made her do, that they would be responsible for her—and that they would place her in a boarding school and that Mr. Salvator would watch over her; where she would be educated at their joint expense. As for me, to put a little balm on my poor heart, they offered me a twelve hundred pound income as a pension. Mr. Salvator responded in the name of the group and they took Rose Noel away.

MR. JACKAL

Where?

LA BROCANTI

But I just told you, I don't know.

MR. JACKAL

You think rightly that I won't take this on your word?

(He lights his cellar light.)

LA BROCANTI

What are you going to do?

MR. JACKAL

A little domestic visit to see if you haven't hidden the child in some corner.

LA BROCANTI

Mr. Jackal, when I swear to you—

MR. JACKAL

You know the more you swear, the less I will believe you.

GIBASSIER

(aside) It seems to me it's time to decamp.

MR. JACKAL

Let's look in this closet first.

LA BROCANTI

You will see her poor bed, which they left me, as it wasn't worth the trouble to be taken.

MR. JACKAL

Nothing! Let's visit the little attic.

GIBASSIER

(removing his slippers and hauling himself to the roof) Has he got a nose!

LA BROCANTI

(coughing) Hum! Hum!

MR. JACKAL

You are catching a cold, Brocanti, I'm warning you, not surprising the skylight's open! Huh! To whom do those legs belong?

GIBASSIER

To someone who knows how to use them—happily.

(He disappears over the roof.)

MR. JACKAL

(pushing half his body out the skylight) Sir! Sir! My word, bon voyage!

(shuts the skylight) Wait, he left his shoes.

(taking a slipper and examines it) If that brigand of a Gibassier wasn't in the galleys, I would say it was his foot. Let's keep this specimen like a piece of evidence. It's probable that one day or another, I will have a bone to pick with this big bloke.

(takes his Gazette from his pocket) *Star-Evening Paper.*

(wrapping the shoes) Who can ever deny the utility of the news-papers?

(who puts them in his pocket) Now, us two, Brocanti! Wait, someone is coming up the stairs.

BABOLIN

(on the stairway) Brocanti! Eh! La Brocanti!

LA BROCANTI

Who's coming here again, this poltroon, at such an hour.

BABOLIN

(closer) Here's an event—a terrible one.

MR. JACKAL

Not a word of me, you understand, Brocanti?

LA BROCANTI

Oh, my God, my God—what a night!

BABOLIN

(enters) A chair, a chair, and a cushion. I am going to be sick, like Rose Noel.

LA BROCANTI

Look—what's wrong with you? Speak imbecile! I thought I was rid of you.

BABOLIN

You haven't the least drop of something? Of kirsch or a love potion?

LA BROCANTI

(pulling him by the arm) Will you speak?

BABOLIN

Oh la la! Oh la la!

MR. JACKAL

(listening) He was marvelously able to listen to all we said, that gentleman.

LA BROCANTI

But what's wrong with you? Speak!

BABOLIN

Well, Rose Noel has been carried off.

LA BROCANTI

What do you mean carried off? And by whom?

MR. JACKAL

(to himself) Carried off? That complicates matters.

LA BROCANTI

By whom, I ask you?

BABOLIN

By one of the four gentlemen from the other day, probably.

LA BROCANTI

And how do you know she was carried off?

BABOLIN

Luck, pure luck!

LA BROCANTI

But will you get to the point?

BABOLIN

Oh! Don't eat your blood—we are going to tell you in two words. I was crossing the place Maubert, I thought I heard the glass break in a carriage and my name, Babolin, Babolin! I recognized the voice of Rose Noel. I turned and a paper fell at my feet. I took it and I escaped. Next moment, a gentleman jumped onto the pavement and ran after me. I made two or three dodges. That was the distance. A gentleman jumped to the pavement and tried to run after me. Outran him. Rose Noel cried for help, but you understand, Brocanti, at 2:00 in the morning on the place Maubert, there wasn't a crowd. The gentleman got back in the carriage and whipped the coachman toward the Rue St. Jacques! Seeing that no one ran after me, I stopped, I clambered up a street lamp and I read, "They are kidnapping me, Mr. Salvator, save me. Rose Noel" written in a hurry on a scrap of paper. I ran to Rue Mason #4—Mr. Salvator's—to wake him for it wasn't long, he was already dressed. "Rose Noel kidnapped?" he cried, "Quickly! Quickly!" "Where are you going?" I asked him. "To find Mr. Jackal. He's the only one who can get her back," he said.

MR. JACKAL

(aside) There's a flatterer.

BABOLIN

Good. Only Mr. Jackal wasn't there, Brocanti. You know he's like the bat, he leaves at night and doesn't return until morning.

LA BROCANTI

You intend to shut up, wretch!

BABOLIN

Why should I shut up? "Then," Mr. Salvator said, "let's go to Brocanti. She may perhaps know something." I told him in reply, "I don't think so, but never mind. Come anyway. I'll run ahead to get lights."

MR. JACKAL

(coming down) Then get lights, imbecile, since you came for that.

BABOLIN

(aside) Mr. Jackal, where can I hide?

MR. JACKAL

(taking the candle) This way, Mr. Salvator. This way.

(Mr. Salvator enters.)

SALVATOR

Mr. Jackal, I was looking for you.

MR. JACKAL

I know it.

SALVATOR

Rose Noel has been kidnapped.

MR. JACKAL

I know it.

SALVATOR

What is to be done?

MR. JACKAL

Where was she?

SALVATOR

At the pension of Madame Desmarest, at Vanvres.

MR. JACKAL

Then to the pension of Madame Desmarest.

SALVATOR

Ah, Mr. Jackal, if you find her.

MR. JACKAL

I hope indeed to get her back—I must find her—where can we get a carriage?

SALVATOR

I have one below.

MR. JACKAL

In that case, en route.

(He lights her hand lamp.)

BABOLIN

(coming from under the table and following them) Good! I will be right behind you! You didn't see that in your cards, Mother?

(He leaves behind Salvator and Jackal.)

LA BROCANTI

(alone) Oh—what night! What a night! Hopefully, they'll continue to pay my pension.

CURTAIN

ACT III

SCENE 5

The Courtyard of the pension of Madame Desmarest. At the right a large wall which extends and is lost in the trees. To the left, the pavilion in which Rose Noel's chamber is situated, visible to the public. The door of this room faces opposite the entry gate. Window in the rear. Small bed of pensioner, slippers at the foot of the bed, candle on a table. At the rear, a house whose windows give on the garden of the pension. It is around 7:00 in the morning.

SALVATOR and BABOLIN

(outside at the gate) Hey somebody—hey! hey!

BABOLIN

Wait, Mr. Salvator. I am going to climb a tree.

(climbing) I'm up. I can see the interior of the house.

SALVATOR

Well?

BABOLIN

One would say it's the Castle of Sleeping Beauty. No one is stirring. Knock—keep it up—someone must come!

SALVATOR

(rapping) Hey! Hey!

BABOLIN

Want me to come down and let you in?

SALVATOR

Eh! Wretch—it's breaking and entering you are proposing.

BABOLIN

Then knock!

(Salvator knocks)

SALVATOR

Ah, there's a door opening.

BABOLIN

Ah, good idea! Good day, sir!

SALVATOR

Madame Desmarest! Madame Desmarest!

PIERRE

Hey—up there! Who do you want, at such an hour!

BABOLIN

Open the door. We're going to tell you.

SALVATOR

Open! Open!

PIERRE

First of all—who are you?

SALVATOR

I am Salvator, the tutor of the young girl who was put in pension here day before yesterday.

BABOLIN

Ah! Mr. Salvator! There a window in the house which is blinking and opening. I see inside an old woman.

MADAME DESMAREST

(from her window) What is it, Pierre?

PIERRE

Madame, it's the tutor of Miss Rose Noel, who insists on speaking to you.

SALVATOR

Immediately, Madame! And on a matter of the highest importance.

MADAME DESMAREST

Open, Pierre, I'm coming down.

SALVATOR

(entering) Thanks, my friend.

PIERRE

Can I shut the door again?

SALVATOR

Useless. I'm waiting for someone, but you can go back inside, my friend. I will watch to see no one comes in or leaves.

BABOLIN

And I, I will give warning!

MADAME DESMAREST

You're asking for Rose Noel?

SALVATOR

Rather, Madame, I've come because of her.

MADAME DESMAREST

Must I wake her?

SALVATOR

She isn't here.

MADAME DESMAREST

What do you mean?

SALVATOR

That she was carried off during the night.

MADAME DESMAREST

Impossible! I escorted her at 9:00 p.m. last night to her room or rather I left her with Miss Suzanne de Valgeneuse.

SALVATOR

Well, I repeat, Madame, she isn't in the room you escorted her to.

MADAME DESMAREST

And are you certain?

SALVATOR

Read this letter which I received at three o'clock in the morning.

MADAME DESMAREST

(after having read) Oh, sir, what can be done?

SALVATOR

Wait and watch, so no one can penetrate either the room, or the court or the garden.

MADAME DESMAREST

Wait for whom?

SALVATOR

The police officer who stopped at the Mayor's to warn him to hold himself ready at the first call.

MADAME DESMAREST

What, sir, is the law coming?

SALVATOR

Without any doubt.

MADAME DESMAREST

Here?

SALVATOR

Here.

MADAME DESMAREST

But if such a thing happens, my establishment is ruined.

SALVATOR

What do you want me to do? It's up to you to watch your pensioners.

MADAME DESMAREST

But, sir, this carrying off is impossible. The walls are higher, the windows solidly shut, if Rose Noel was kidnapped against her will, she must have cried out, and I would have heard her as I live above her.

SALVATOR

Well, Madame, there are ladders for the tallest walls, jimmies for the best locked windows, and gags for young girls' mouths.

MADAME DESMAREST

Shall we go into Rose Noel's room, sir?

SALVATOR

On the contrary, Madame, we are forbidden to enter it, for fear of erasing evidence of the rape.

MADAME DESMAREST

Let's look in the garden, then, perhaps we can see how someone got through the window.

SALVATOR

Pardon, Madame, but entry to the garden is forbidden to everyone.

MADAME DESMAREST

Even to me?

SALVATOR

To you just like the rest, Madame.

MADAME DESMAREST

But still, sir, I am in my own home.

SALVATOR

You are mistaken, Madame. At this time, the law is at your home, and wherever it is, the law is at home.

BABOLIN

(from the top of the wall) Mr. Jackal! There's Mr. Jackal.

MADAME DESMAREST

Who is Mr. Jackal?

SALVATOR

The police officer we are waiting for, Madame.

MR. JACKAL

Do you intend to get down from your perch, scoundrel?

BABOLIN

Right away; Mr. Jackal, right away.

(Jackal enters humming—without paying attention to anyone, he tours the court. Babolin hides in the corner of the door.)

MADAME DESMAREST

Sir.

MR. JACKAL

Madame Desmarest, I suppose? Very good.

(he continues to hum) Where is Miss Rose Noel's room?

MADAME DESMAREST

There it is, sir.

MR. JACKAL

Whose house is that which gives on your garden?

MADAME DESMAREST

That of Mr. Gérard.

MR. JACKAL

Oh! Oh! Mr. Gérard. The honest man. Isn't that the way he's

known?

MADAME DESMAREST

Ah, sir, he deserves it greatly.

MR. JACKAL

Who before coming to Vanvres lived at Viry sur Orge?

MADAME DESMAREST

I believe so.

MR. JACKAL

And I, I am sure of it.

(He starts humming again.)

SALVATOR

Gérard! That's the name that had such an effect on Rose Noel the other day.

(to Madame Desmarest) Is Mr. Gérard married?

MADAME DESMAREST

No, sir.

SALVATOR

Do you know someone around Mr. Gérard who bears the name "Orsola?"

MR. JACKAL

Dead at least seven years, killed by a dog—let's get back to business. What does this wall give on?

MADAME DESMAREST

On a small deserted street.

MR. JACKAL

Go outside, Mr. Salvator, run along the wall and see if you don't find at the base of the wall, some bit of plaster fallen off. If you do, note its place.

SALVATOR

Be easy.

BABOLIN

Would you like me to go with you, Mr. Salvator?

SALVATOR

Come!

MR. JACKAL

Now, just the two of us, Madame.

MADAME DESMAREST

Question me, sir, and I am ready to reply.

MR. JACKAL

At what time to your pensioners go to bed?

MADAME DESMAREST

At eight o'clock in the winter.

MR. JACKAL

And the sub-mistresses?

MADAME DESMAREST

At nine o'clock.

MR. JACKAL

And you, Madame, at what time did you go to sleep yesterday?

MADAME DESMAREST

At ten o'clock, sir.

MR. JACKAL

And you saw nothing, heard nothing?

MADAME DESMAREST

Saw nothing, heard nothing.

MR. JACKAL

Then, you noticed nothing unusual.

MADAME DESMAREST

Nothing unusual.

MR. JACKAL

Nothing unusual! That's unusual.

SALVATOR

(pointing to the tile from the wall) This is what you want.

MR. JACKAL

My word, yes. You marked the place carefully!

SALVATOR

Exactly.

BABOLIN

And there, I threw a stone, to the side of the wall.

MR. JACKAL

Let's go there or rather let me go there first by myself. Ah! Ah!
Here are traces of footprints of the same length and a larger
one—could a single man have done this?

SALVATOR

No.

MR. JACKAL

What makes you think that?

SALVATOR

The prints are arranged differently. One of the two men leaned
on his right foot—the footprint of the right foot is deeper than
that of the left.

MR. JACKAL

Have you been in the profession, Mr. Salvator?

SALVATOR

No, but I've done some hunting.

MR. JACKAL

Look here.

SALVATOR

What?

MR. JACKAL

A ray of light.

(He pulls out of his pocket the shoes of Gibassier.)

SALVATOR

What's that?

VICTOR

A lobster clue, I bet!

MR. JACKAL

(measuring the impression) Exactly the same. The same position of the nails. No need to bother about this one, I've got him.

PIERRE

You mean you've got his slippers.

MR. JACKAL

You will learn, my good friend, that when I have the shoe, I have the foot and when I have the foot, I have the rest of him. Turn to the other. Ah—ah—here's a third track. A very particular foot which has no resemblance to that we just examined—a foot of a great lord or churchman.

SALVATOR

A man of the world, Mr. Jackal.

MR. JACKAL

Why do you stress a man of the world?

SALVATOR

Because in our day, churchmen don't wear spurs—and here at the heel is the little cut made by a spur.

MR. JACKAL

You are right, on my word! Now, let's see where these foot-prints go and where they come from. Ah, here they go from the wall to the window and from the window to the wall. It appears the ravishers were well informed. Ah, come here, Mr. Salvator! Look!

SALVATOR

Two tracks in the ground joined by a line cutting them.

MR. JACKAL

You recognize the signs of a ladder.

SALVATOR

And the first step is pushed into the muddy ground—caused by the humidity.

MR. JACKAL

It must be a pleasure to work with you, Mr. Salvator. No—it's a question of figuring out how many men leaned on the ladder to cause it sink in the mud thus deeply. Is there a ladder in the house, Madame Desmarest?

MADAME DESMAREST

Ask Pierre.

SALVATOR

Mr. Pierre, do you have a ladder?

PIERRE

Ah! Good question.

MR. JACKAL

Reply to it.

PIERRE

Certainly, I have a ladder.

MR. JACKAL

And where is this ladder?

PIERRE

It's near the greenhouse.

MR. JACKAL

(pointing to a ladder leaning against Gérard's house) You must be mistaken, my friend, wouldn't that be it, by chance?

PIERRE

Goodness—yes! Who the devil took my ladder and put it under Mr. Gérard's window? Now do you want it? I am going to go get it.

MR. JACKAL

No. I am going there myself. That's what complicates things. Your Mr. Gérard passes for rich, doesn't he?

MADAME DESMAREST

They say he's a millionaire.

MR. JACKAL

Did my comedians kill two birds with one stone? This will have to be looked into—but later.

(fitting the ladder to the prints) Already we have a piece of proof. The marks and the ladder are in agreement.

SALVATOR

And what's more remarkable is that the ladder isn't of ordinary dimensions.

MR. JACKAL

Do you have a son, Pierre?

PIERRE

Yes. Who told you that?

MR. JACKAL

Between twelve and fifteen?

PIERRE

He'll be fourteen soon.

MR. JACKAL

Soon! It is indeed his son.

PIERRE

What do you mean, it's indeed his son?

MR. JACKAL

He needed help from a child to show him the way and he brought a large ladder, so the child could go up the ladder at the same time with him.

PIERRE

Well, so what? Is there anything wrong in that?

MR. JACKAL

No—on the contrary! Come here, my friend—how long is it since you worked in the garden?

PIERRE

Not for at least three days.

MR. JACKAL

Then for three days your ladder has been near the greenhouse.

PIERRE

It isn't near the greenhouse, as you just placed it here.

MR. JACKAL

This boy is smart! But there is one thing of which I am sure—it's that he had no experience in kidnapping. Come up with me, my friend!

(Pierre gives a questioning look to Madame Desmarest.)

MADAME DESMAREST

Do what the gentleman tells you, Pierre.

(Pierre climbs.)

MR. JACKAL

Again.

(to Salvator) Well?

SALVATOR

It's stuck in but not the other side.

MR. JACKAL

Go down, my friend.

PIERRE

I'm down.

MR. JACKAL

Notice how this man says few things but what he says is well said. Now, my friend, take Madame Desmarest in your arms.

PIERRE

Fie! Sir!

MR. JACKAL

Take Madame Desmarest in your arms.

MADAME DESMAREST

But what are you saying?

PIERRE

I will never dare, sir.

MADAME DESMAREST

I forbid you to, Pierre.

MR. JACKAL

(coming down the ladder) Go where I was, my friend.

(He intends to carry off Madame Desmarest.)

MADAME DESMAREST

But, sir, but, sir, what are you doing?

MR. JACKAL

Suppose, Madame, that I am in love with you.

PIERRE

Now, there's a supposition.

MADAME DESMAREST

But sir!

MR. JACKAL

Relax, Madame, it's only as my friend, Pierre, said—a supposition. I am carrying you off—rather I am not—I am going to help you to climb, Much prefer that. Fear nothing.

(they go up)

(to Salvator) Is it pressing in on the other side?

SALVATOR

Not at all.

MR. JACKAL

(to Babolin) Come here to make it balance.

BABOLIN

Me?

MR. JACKAL

Yes, you—get on the second rung.

BABOLIN

There.

SALVATOR

The ladder is exactly on the same point as the other.

MR. JACKAL

Then everything is done. Let's get down.

MADAME DESMAREST

I do not understand.

MR. JACKAL

It's very simple, now. You are somewhat heavier than Rose Noel.

(to Babolin) How much do you weigh?

BABOLIN

Sixty-five pounds. I weighed myself three days ago.

MR. JACKAL

The two men who kidnapped Rose Noel were sixty-five pounds heavier than Pierre and me.

BABOLIN

He's clever, this Mr. Jackal! He's clever.

PIERRE

Ah, I understand now. Someone kidnapped one of the pensioners.

MR. JACKAL

Madame Desmarest—never lose this boy—he's a treasure of penetration. Let's look around the interior of the room.

(to Madame Desmarest) You have a double key for each room?

MADAME DESMAREST

Here's that of Rose Noel.

(Jackal opens the door. They all try to enter.)

MR. JACKAL

Softly! All depends on the first examination. Ah! Ah! Traces of footprints from the door to the bed—and from the bed to the window. Mr. Salvator—look with your hunter's eyes.

SALVATOR

Ah! Ah! Something new. A woman's footprint. It's outlined by the garden gravel.

MR. JACKAL

What did I always tell you, Mr. Salvator? "Cherchez la femme," this time the woman is found.

MADAME DESMAREST

What do you mean, the woman is found? You think there's a woman in this affair?

MR. JACKAL

There's a woman in every case. Rather than having a report given, I say "look for the woman." They look for the woman and when the woman is found—

MADAME DESMAREST

Well.

MR. JACKAL

—there's no delay in finding the man. One day, a roofing man fell from a roof and broke both of his legs. They gave me a report and I said "look for the woman." That made them laugh. I questioned the injured man. The imbecile was amusing himself watching a grisette undress in her garret. He missed his step and he fell. Let's look for the woman, Mr. Salvator, let's look for the woman.

SALVATOR

This one is a coquette. She followed the garden paths so as not to dirty her slippers. Yellow gravel, without a mixture of mud.

MR. JACKAL

When you stop being an errand-boy, Mr. Salvator, come tell me. And now, Madame Desmarest that's what happened. You yourself conducted Ms. Rose Noel to her chamber.

MADAME DESMAREST

Myself, sir.

MR. JACKAL

She was very sad.

MADAME DESMAREST

How do you know that?

MR. JACKAL

It's not difficult to figure out. Her handkerchief was wet, she went to bed crying. They knocked on the door.

MADAME DESMAREST

Which one did that?

MR. JACKAL

Probably the woman. Rose Noel got up and opened the door.

MADAME DESMAREST

Without knowing who was knocking?

MR. JACKAL

Who told you she didn't know who was knocking? Behind the woman came the young man with boots and spurs. Behind the young man were the men with large shoes. She was overpowered. They put a kerchief in her mouth—they threw her peignoir over her from the bed and wrapped her in it—and thus, they carried her off. See, they took her by way of the window—and the proof that she came through the window and not very willingly—?

SALVATOR

Is that she grabbed the curtain and that the curtain is torn.

MR. JACKAL

The rest goes by itself—they went over the wall. The woman returned to the room. She closed the window, very naturally, then the door, then she went back to sleep.

SALVATOR

(grasping the hand of Mr. Jackal) I've got it all—let me do it. Madame Desmarest can you get us a slipper of Miss Suzanne de Valgeneuse without her knowing it?

MADAME DESMAREST

Probably. She probably put them outside her door yesterday evening so her chambermaid could clean them as usual.

SALVATOR

Then Madame Desmarest—a slipper of Miss Suzanne's and not a word.

MR. JACKAL

You hear, Madame, not a word.

MADAME DESMAREST

I am going there myself.

(She leaves.)

SALVATOR

Mr. Pierre, if you want to go back to your room we have no further need of you. Babolin, if you want to go play with your top, you will be pleasing us.

BABOLIN

I have no top, Mr. Salvator.

SALVATOR

Then go buy one—here's for it.

(He give him five francs.)

BABOLIN

Oh—a five franc note.

(Babolin leaves but Pierre stops by his door.)

PIERRE

Why should I go back to my room? I only take orders from Madame Desmarest.

SALVATOR

The woman is Miss Suzanne de Valgeneuse. The man with spurs is her brother.

MR. JACKAL

You think so?

SALVATOR

I am sure of it. She was the one who suggested the pension of Madame Desmarest for Rose Noel that day at Pétrus's. It was she who fought all my objections at the instigation of her brother. From that moment, the plan for the kidnapping was made. Ah, my dear cousins.

MR. JACKAL

What do you mean there?

SALVATOR

Nothing—I say you are a great man, Mr. Jackal and that your maxim "cherchez la femme" will pass on to posterity.

MADAME DESMAREST

(entering) Here's one of Miss Suzanne's slippers, gentlemen.

SALVATOR

(measuring the footprint) Sir! Well—what do you say to that?

MR. JACKAL

I say that it is Miss Suzanne who's behind all this. Madame Desmarest, call Miss Suzanne.

MADAME DESMAREST

Wait, sir, here she is.

MR. JACKAL

Where's that?

MADAME DESMAREST

She's walking toward the garden.

MR. JACKAL

Signal her to come here.

MADAME DESMAREST

I don't know if she will come.

MR. JACKAL

And why wouldn't she come?

MADAME DESMAREST

Because Miss Suzanne is very proud.

MR. JACKAL

Call her anyway. If she doesn't come. I'll go fetch her.

MADAME DESMAREST

Miss Suzanne! Miss Suzanne!

SUZANNE

Madame does me the honor of calling me, I believe?

(Mr. Jackal is in the court; Salvator in the pavilion—invisible to Suzanne.)

MADAME DESMAREST

Yes, my child, for here's a gentleman, who wishes to ask you some questions.

SUZANNE

Some questions from me? But I don't know the gentleman.

MADAME DESMAREST

The gentleman is the representative of the authorities.

SUZANNE

What have I do with the authorities?

MADAME DESMAREST

Calm yourself, my child; it's a question of Rose Noel.

SUZANNE

Well—so what?

MR. JACKAL

So what? Please leave us, Madame Desmarest, and bid Mr. Pierre to go to his room.

(Pierre and Madame Desmarest both leave.)

MR. JACKAL

So what, Miss—? We want to have some information about your friend.

SUZANNE

What friend?

MR. JACKAL

Miss Rose Noel.

SUZANNE

I choose my friends from places other than the streets. Miss Rose Noel was perhaps my protégé but she was not my friend.

MR. JACKAL

Then I am simply going to interrogate you.

SUZANNE

Interrogate me? About what?

MR. JACKAL

On the kidnapping of Miss Rose Noel.

SUZANNE

Oh! Poor little thing—she was kidnapped?

MR. JACKAL

You know it better than anyone, Miss, since you participated in the kidnapping.

SUZANNE

You are mad, sir.

MR. JACKAL

No, Miss—I am—

(opens his coat and show his uniform)

SUZANNE

Why didn't you say so before? One would have answered you with the respect due to your rank.

MR. JACKAL

Let's not waste any more time, Miss. Your name and station in the world?

SUZANNE

Then this really is an interrogation?

MR. JACKAL

Yes, Miss.

SUZANNE

My name! I am Aimée Adélaîde Suzanne de Valgeneuse. I

am the daughter of the Marquise René de Valgeneuse, peer of France, niece of Louis Clement de Valgeneuse, Cardinal at the Court of Rome and sister of the Count Loredan de Valgeneuse, lieutenant in the guards. I am the heiress of a half-million pound income. There—

MR. JACKAL

(taking a step back and rebuttoning his coat) Pardon, Miss, I was unaware.

SUZANNE

Yes, I understand, you were unaware that I am my father's daughter, my uncle's niece and my brother's sister. But now you know it—don't forget it.

(She makes a disdainful gesture with her hand and starts to leave.)

MR. JACKAL

Pardon, Miss, one more word, I beg you. You are proud and boastful of your fortune—but this fortune comes to you through the succession of an uncle whose will they say, disappeared. Reduced to misery by the disappearance of this will, Mr. Conrad de Valgeneuse killed himself—but let's suppose for a moment that your cousin is not dead and the will is found. You would be ruined—you, and your brother.

SUZANNE

Is that a threat you are making me?

MR. JACKAL

No, Miss—it's an opinion I'm giving you.

SUZANNE

From where do you get an opinion in this?

MR. JACKAL

The opinion is not in what I've told you, but in what I still have to tell you. Listen to me then, Miss, and although I speak quietly to you—don't lose one of my words for they are the words of a friend.

SUZANNE

(scornfully) You, a friend?

MR. JACKAL

You shall judge—the young girl your brother had kidnapped and who he thinks is a gypsy is not a gypsy—she is the niece of Mr. Gérard—and on the day her uncle dies, she will inherit five million. So your brother must not make her his mistress—but his wife. Will you say this advice doesn't come from a friend?

SUZANNE

I don't know from whom it comes nor from what motive it is given, but it is good. In an hour, I will leave to join my brother— and I swear to you that Rose Noel will never be his mistress— goodbye, sir!

(Mr. Jackal bows very low.)

MR. JACKAL

Your humble servant, Miss.

(Suzanne leaves.)

MR. JACKAL

Mr. Salvator, I believe we have nothing more of importance to do here and as I have a different reason for staying, I won't keep you.

SALVATOR

If I asked you for an explanation, Mr. Jackal, would you give me one?

MR. JACKAL

No, Mr. Salvator.

SALVATOR

Well, I will give one myself. You're afraid of this viper, Mr. Jackal.

MR. JACKAL

I'm not afraid of anything, Mr. Salvator.

SALVATOR

Well, Mr. Jackal, what you don't want to do, I will do myself.

MR. JACKAL

You?

SALVATOR

Me! Only one last word—is it your conscience which forces you to abstain from acting?

MR. JACKAL

It's my duty—goodbye, Mr. Conrad.

SALVATOR

(turning quickly) Mr. Conrad?

MR. JACKAL

Pardon, I made a mistake—goodbye, Mr. Salvator.

SALVATOR

Mr. Jackal within eight hours I will have found Rose Noel and brought her back.

MR. JACKAL

If that happens try to protect her.

SALVATOR

Oh—once in my hands, she'll never leave them. Goodbye, Mr. Jackal. I'll answer for that.

(Salvator leaves.)

MR. JACKAL

Man proposes—God disposes. While waiting, let's see why this ladder was placed against Gérard's window—if that brigand Gibassier wasn't in Toulon, I would swear it was he who did this.

CURTAIN

ACT III

SCENE 6

Interior of Gérard's room at Vanvres. The most complete disorder—chairs overturned—secretary forced open—light continuing to burn on the right table—a bloody knife on the furniture. Jackal is outside on the ladder. Only his arm can be seen which passes through a broken pane of glass feeling for the lock—he opens the lock and then in the window Jackal appears.

VOICE

(from outside the door)

Mr. Gérard! Mr. Gérard! Open up, Mr. Gérard—open up.

MR. JACKAL

(at the window) It's very imprudent for a millionaire to sleep on the first floor without grills on his windows—true, it gives on the pension of young girls—but the sheep attract the wolves.

(he jumps into the room) Here's a beautiful mess! Perhaps it is an effect of art.

VOICE

Mr. Gérard—if you don't reply I am going to get the police.

MR. JACKAL

Go without wasting a moment. That's what you ought best to do.

VOICE

(frightened, going off) There's someone in Mr. Gérard's room. Help, police—police!

MR. JACKAL

That's very good! One of the three men has separated himself. The one whose shoes I have in my pocket, he came with the ladder, leaned on it underneath the window, broke a pane and entered. Mr. Gérard slept or didn't sleep. The bed is made, but seems not to be in its place. Why isn't it in place? Oh—because they moved it to force open the armoire which was behind it. Mr. Gérard heard a noise, he came in, he was overcome, since here is the desk forced open—the drawer is empty.

(seeing a spot on the floor and putting his handkerchief over it) That's clear. A piece of evidence. To the stationhouse.

(while rummaging he spots the knife) What do I see shining under it? Oh—oh—here's something will put us on the man's track. "Lardereau to Valence." Near to the road to Toulon. Gibassier escaped from the galleys. It was his legs I saw at Brocanti's. These are his shoes in my pocket and this is his knife which I have in my hand. More evidence. To the stationhouse.

(a noise is heard) God. They've come back.

VOICE

(outside) In the name of the law—open.

MR. JACKAL

Nice voice? Who is Commissioner in Vanvres? It's Henry
Bertin, one of my proteges. I am charmed to see that I used my
protection so well.

COMMISSIONER

In the name of the law—open.

MR. JACKAL

What the devil has become of Mr. Gérard in all this?

(opening the door of the cabinet) Well—there he is—the assassin
placed him here—he put the key in his pocket and left by the
door, locked it from outside and got to the street by the window
on the street floor.

(He goes to the cabinet; meanwhile the door is forced; the
Commissioner rushes in the room with police; at this moment
Mr. Jackal comes out of the cabinet pulling Mr. Gérard's body
by the shoulder.)

COMMISSIONER

(pointing to Mr. Jackal) Arrest this man!

MR. JACKAL

Whom do you wish to arrest?

COMMISSIONER

You, by God.

MR. JACKAL

Ah, dear Mr. Henry, I had a high opinion of you and now you destroy it yourself.

COMMISSIONER

Mr. Jackal.

ALL

Mr. Jackal.

MR. JACKAL

Let's see, help me to put this brave Mr. Gérard on his bed. I have to be at the Prefect's at eight o'clock and I want to know before I go if he is dead or alive. If he's not dead he's in very bad condition. Is there a doctor in the village?

COMMISSIONER

Yes, but I saw him leave this morning in his carriage.

MR. JACKAL

Then, as there is no time to lose, send for a priest.

COMMISSIONER

Today is Sunday, he is singing a mass at the chapel of Mr. Lamotte Houden. But I saw a monk on his way to Meudon, where two lovers asphyxiated themselves. I will go—

MR. JACKAL

No, not you.

GENDARME

I am going, sir.

MR. JACKAL

If you find a doctor in Meudon, bring him along.

(The gendarme leaves.)

MR. JACKAL

There, now that you have seen all there is to see, my good friends, let's have some air. If Mr. Gérard is dead he doesn't need you here, if he's alive it's our business not yours.

ASSISTANTS

(slowly as they leave) Oh! Try to preserve him for us, Mr. Jackal, you don't know the good he has done in the country—he is the father of the poor. We are going to pray to God for him.

MR. JACKAL

You will do well! Go, my friends, go. Watch the door and don't let anyone enter except the monk and the doctor—

(the gendarmes leave—to Commissioner) As for you—take notes for your report.

COMMISSIONER

Do you want to dictate it to me?

MR. JACKAL

I don't have the time. I should already be on my way to Paris.

(The Commissioner sets to work at a table.)

COMMISSIONER

Sunday, etc., etc.

MR. JACKAL

(about to leave) Hush! It seems to me that I heard a sigh. Come help me, Mr. Henry.

(they listen to Gérard) Ah—ah—it appears he's calling us.

GÉRARD

Ah!

MR. JACKAL

Bravo! 7:10. I will spur the horse.

(he takes a silver spoon from the glass on the desk)

It appears the desk was well furnished; although made of silver, the little spoon was scorned.

(He puts some drops of red liquor contained in a flask which he has about him, and helps Gérard to drink.)

GÉRARD

(returning to himself) Thanks, Mr. Thief, thanks.

MR. JACKAL

Honest, Mr. Gérard, it's not a case of a thief here but justice watching over you.

GÉRARD

(returning to himself) J—J—Justice?

MR. JACKAL

See how Justice reassures him! Relax, dear Mr. Gérard; we are old acquaintances, what the devil. I took your deposition after the murder at Viry sur Orge, which resulted in the indictment against Mr. Sarranti and caused him to be condemned to death as a thief and assassin.

GÉRARD

I have nothing to say except to a confessor.

MR. JACKAL

You are going to be served as you wish. I have sent for a priest and a doctor.

GÉRARD

Oh, the priest first, the priest first.

(He falls back on his bed.)

MR. JACKAL

The devil! And I have to leave him. My dear Mr. Henry, I doubt that Mr. Gérard will revive, but if he does, do me the favor of watching him and informing me of his gestures and actions.

COMMISSIONER

Of the acts and gestures of the honest Mr. Gérard?

MR. JACKAL

Yes, of the good Mr. Gérard.

COMMISSIONER

You have some intentions with regard to him then?

MR. JACKAL

Hush! I'm preparing a surprise for him. Don't breathe a word of it to him. Only if he is ill, make him drink a cup of this liquor; it will sustain him for a while; 7:15, luckily what I am bringing will excuse my delay. Goodbye.

Mr. Henry! Goodbye.

(An agent comes in.)

AGENT

From the Prefect.

MR. JACKAL

From the Prefect?

AGENT

Yes—it seems it's about a grave concern, for he ordered me not to return without you.

MR. JACKAL

My, my, my—here's something else! Mr. Sarranti has returned to France. I thought to arrest him the other day at Bordiers—and he is coming to surrender himself. Does this imbecile of an honest man, who was all right in India, who could easily have stayed there, imagine he can return and purge his guilt? Poor devil—I feel sorry for him!

(to Agent) Come! Come! And you, dear Mr. Henry—don't forget my instructions.

(looking at Gérard) Decidedly, I wouldn't give them for nothing.

(Jackal leaves with the agent.)

GÉRARD

(reopening his eyes) He is gone? This man frightens me! What is this letter he has received? I heard him pronounce the name of Sarranti. Oh—how weak I am! Help! I am dying.

COMMISSIONER

What's wrong, dear Mr. Gérard?

GÉRARD

Mr. Henry Bertin. Do you think they can find a priest, sir?

A POLICEMAN

(entering) Pardon, excuse me, Mr. Commissioner—it's the monk—my partner and I met him on the way from Meudon and he sent us ahead, waiting for the doctor.

GÉRARD

(rising up) The monk! What monk?

COMMISSIONER

The Curé of Vanvres is away—and since I knew that a monk was at Meudon, I sent for him. It seems they met him on the way.

GÉRARD

Then—then this monk is a stranger to the country?

(Enter Dominique.)

DOMINIQUE

(replying to Gérard's question) I've come from Rome where I have been received into orders by the hands of His Holiness himself.

GÉRARD

That's good. Coming from Rome perhaps you have great power. Closer, come closer, Father.

DOMINIQUE

Here I am.

GÉRARD

It seems to me you are very young.

DOMINIQUE

I am not offering myself, sir, I have been requested.

GÉRARD

I only mean that at your age, one has not perhaps meditated enough on the somber side of life to reply to the questions that I am going to put to you.

DOMINIQUE

All that I can reply to you, sir, is that if you question my faith, I will reply in faith, and if you question my spirit, well, I will reply spiritually.

GÉRARD

That's fine, Father. Gentlemen—leave us.

(Everyone leaves.)

GÉRARD

Sit down, Father, and come as close to me as possible. I am so weak that I can hardly speak.

(Dominique sits.)

GÉRARD

Now, in the name of heaven—don't be scandalized by what I

tell you and especially promise me not to abandon me before I have told you all that I have to tell you.

DOMINIQUE

Speak with confidence, sir, I am listening.

GÉRARD

You know better than I, the dogmas of religion to which you are born—tell me—is there a case where the words of a dying man can be revealed by the confessor who has received them?

DOMINIQUE

I know of none, sir.

GÉRARD

So once you have received my confession, none could force you to make it public?

DOMINIQUE

Not by anyone in the world.

GÉRARD

Not even by a court, not even by a minister, not even by a King?

DOMINIQUE

Not even by the Vicar of God who sits at Rome.

GÉRARD

And what ought a priest to do who was placed between death and revealing a secret so confided to him?

DOMINIQUE

He must die.

GÉRARD

Then listen to me, Father, hear me.

DOMINIQUE

I am waiting.

GÉRARD

And I, I hesitate. It seems to me that I still have strength and that I can wait. Couldn't you return this evening—or tomorrow?

DOMINIQUE

Impossible! For it is likely I will not only quit Paris, but France, perhaps tomorrow, perhaps tonight even. Never to return.

GÉRARD

(aside) He's leaving—better him than someone else—ah! Ah!

DOMINIQUE

What's wrong?

GÉRARD

Father, Father, I think I am going to die. Help me—there on the table a flask. Be kind enough—a sip of liquor which is in the flask.

DOMINIQUE

I understand.

(he makes Gérard take a sip of the liquor)

It's strange. It seems to me I know this man.

GÉRARD

Listen to me now. I am going to tell you everything succinctly as possible. I'm afraid I won't be able to finish.

DOMINIQUE

(sitting) Speak, I am listening.

GÉRARD

I was living in the country a few leagues from Paris. I lived with a woman thirty years of age—beautiful—too beautiful for my good. She was born in the mountains of the Pyrenees. She had a bitter and obstinate will, and she had brought me her under her will! My brother, who had left for India, left me with his two children, a boy and a girl—had recommended one of his friends as their tutor—a Corsican.

(Dominique passes successively from curiosity to interest and from interest to terror) My brother died.

DOMINIQUE

The place you lived—was it called Viry sur Orge?

GÉRARD

Yes.

DOMINIQUE

Weren't the children called Victor and Leonie?

GÉRARD

Those were their names.

DOMINIQUE

Oh! I recognize you, now, although I only saw you once before while I was suffering severe pain. You are Mr. Gérard.

GÉRARD

Yes, but you—who are you?

DOMINIQUE

Don't you recognize me?

GÉRARD

No!

DOMINIQUE

Have a good look!

GÉRARD

Who are you, in the name of heaven?

DOMINIQUE

I am Dominique Sarranti!

GÉRARD

Oh!

DOMINIQUE

I am the son of Philippe Sarranti, who you accused of murder and theft and who was, by your action, condemned to death, while I was finishing my novitiate.

GÉRARD

My God! My God!

DOMINIQUE

You see well how you would betray yourself if I listen any longer to your confession; because instead of listening with the charity of a priest and the pardon of a Christian, I would listen with the hate of a son whose father you have dishonored and consequently with a curse in his heart.

(He goes quickly to the door.)

GÉRARD

No, no, no! Stay—to the contrary, stay—it is Providence which has sent you. Stay! It is God who will permit me before dying to repair the harm I have done.

DOMINIQUE

You want that? Take care! I ask nothing better than to stay—it took a superhuman effort on my part to tell you who I was and not to abuse the luck that brought me near you.

GÉRARD

No, not luck, but Providence, my brother, Providence. Oh, far from fleeing you, far from fearing you, I had been, before dying, I would have been on top of the world if I'd known how to find you. You here—listen to me, but no, I feel, I won't have the strength to tell you the horrible deed.

DOMINIQUE

But my father? My father?

GÉRARD

Well, one of the children was killed by me, the other—

DOMINIQUE

My father, I tell you?

GÉRARD

But don't you see I am dying?

DOMINIQUE

Oh—don't die, wretch—I need the innocence of my father.

GÉRARD

Yes, your father is innocent.

DOMINIQUE

I knew it—and yet, I might see him die on the scaffold without the power to save him, for despite the admission you have made to me, sir, as the admission is in confession, I cannot reveal it, and the accusation continues to weigh eternally on the head of my father—oh, sir, you are indeed infamous!

GÉRARD

But am I not dying? Do you think that if I didn't feel the mortal wound the horrible secret would ever leave my mouth?

DOMINIQUE

But, you dead, will I be permitted to reveal it?

GÉRARD

All, father, all—didn't I thank Heaven for bringing you to my bed?

DOMINIQUE

But who will believe the declaration of a son in favor of his father?

GÉRARD

Wait—there—there in—the thickness of the wall a secret armoire. Follow the molding of the door. There—you are there. Push! Do you see a manuscript found in three seals?

DOMINIQUE

A manuscript. Here it is! Here it is!

(reading) Here is my confession before God and man—not to be made public before my death—signed, Gérard.

GÉRARD

That paper contains word-for-word the story of my weakness; for now it is forbidden to you to reveal it in all its details, but after my death, I relieve you of the secret of the confessional.

DOMINIQUE

It will be according to your wish—I swear it before God!

GÉRARD

You see, I succumb to emotion; won't you console me with some words of hope?

DOMINIQUE

Sir, perhaps, you need a more powerful intercession before the Lord than mine. But as for me, I pardon you. Now God willingly ratifies the pardon, that as a priest I beg him to cause to descend on your head.

GÉRARD

(in a voice almost unintelligible)

And now, what does there remain for me to do?

DOMINIQUE

Pray.

(He goes out.)

GÉRARD

(alone) Lord! Lord! Have pity on me! Lord! Lord! Receive me in your mercy!

A SERVANT

(introducing Ludovic) Now, sir, you can enter, the priest is gone.

LUDOVIC

It's against custom—after the doctor, the priest—while today, after the priest, the doctor. Let's hope all this portends well for you, Mr. Gérard.

GÉRARD

(in a weak voice) Who's calling me?

LUDOVIC

Eh! The voice is not wheezing. Are you spitting blood?

(Gérard makes a negative sign)

LUDOVIC

Nothing in the lungs consequently. Lividity—from the enormous quantity of blood lost. Let's see the eye. Look at me! A little distraction caused by terror! The wounds now.

GÉRARD

Great God—if I am not going to die!

LUDOVIC

Eh! Eh! I've seen far worse!

GÉRARD

Oh! The monk! The monk! Run after the monk! Bring him back! No—

(weakening) If—

(fainting) This time I am dying.

LUDOVIC

Well—this is a singular illness. You might say he was terrified of being cured!

CURTAIN

ACT IV
SCENE 7

The Park at Viry seen at night. To the left the château cut away. The lake is seen shining brightly through the trees.

Salvator and others come from the wall at right.

SALVATOR

Come on, let's go Roland!

(Roland jumps over the wall, after Roland, Salvator appears at the top of the wall) Very good, Roland.

JEAN TAUREAU

(from the other side of the wall) Well? What do you see, Mr. Salvator?

SALVATOR

A great park and at the back a sort of château.

JEAN TAUREAU

(showing his head) And no one?

SALVATOR

No one.

JEAN TAUREAU

You are sure?

SALVATOR

Roland is barking.

JEAN TAUREAU

It's very true—only watch out for a trap.

SALVATOR

Come down, and tell Sac a Platre to come down in his turn.

JEAN TAUREAU

Well—he isn't up here yet. Come on—slow poke.

(he takes Sac a Platre by the collar and passes him over the wall)
There. That does it. My turn.

(He jumps.)

SALVATOR

Come here, Roland.

(The dog and the three men group around a tree.)

SAC A PLATRE

(in a half voice) But, say Mr. Salvator, I recognize this place.

SALVATOR

You!

JEAN TAUREAU

There's nothing surprising in that, he's from the country.

SAC A PLATRE

Not at all. I am from Savigny—but that means nothing.

SALVATOR

Well, where are we?

SAC A PLATRE

We are in the Park of the Château Viry. I was there several times for Mr. Gérard—I worked for him—poor dear man.

SALVATOR

For Mr. Gérard, you said?

SAC A PLATRE

Yes.

SALVATOR

And near Mr. Gérard, did you know a woman named Orsola?

SAC A PLATRE

I should say so! She was his mistress. He was going to marry her when the famous catastrophe took place.

SALVATOR

What catastrophe?

SAC A PLATRE

That of the children killed—hold, the poor children, I can still see them playing on the lawn. The little boy was called Victor and the little girl, Leonie.

SALVATOR

They are the two children Mr. Sarranti was accused of having killed. Mr. Sarranti was condemned to death in absentia, returned to France and yesterday, unable to endure the infamous accusation which weighed on him, surrendered himself to the authorities. Now, listen here, you who are honest men, instead of submitting him to a jury which would have acquitted him he was deferred here to a military court; in twenty-four hours he will be sentenced; in forty-eight hours executed unless we find proof of his innocence. This proof at all hazards, I've come to look for here. I am going to tell you briefly what hope leads me here. You both know Rose Noel, don't you?

JEAN TAUREAU

The little gypsy.

SAC A PLATRE

I should say we know here.

SALVATOR

Well, Roland and she know each other, too, and my conviction is that Roland played his role in the terrible drama in the month of May 1820, and that Rose Noel is one of the two children Mr. Sarranti is accused of having killed.

JEAN TAUREAU

That would be a providence.

SALVATOR

Through misfortune, Rose Noel whom I wish to question, was kidnapped on the day after we put her in pension at Vanvres, and by another misfortune I was not able to follow her ravisher. Well, this morning, I said to myself, "Let's use Roland's intelligence and the courage of my good friends of Jean Taureau and Sac a Platre." I brought you to the place where I had found Roland and said to him, "Find!" and he led us to the foot of this wall, which he tried to scale. Here we are on the other side of the wall. Sac a Platre recognizes the garden of this château. It was the château inhabited by Orsola and Mr. Gérard, meaning the two persons whose names made Rose Noel faint. Roland recognized it, too, since he absolutely wants me to leave to let him search. Now what are we going to see? What are we going to find? There's something profoundly funereal in the aspect of all we see. I would be very surprised if some horrible crime wasn't committed here, in fact, the shadow is darker here than elsewhere. The light is weaker than elsewhere—never mind! Let's continue to seek the cause of all this.

JEAN TAUREAU

Silence—it seems to me I heard the step of a horse.

SAC A PLATRE

He's passing by the foot of this wall which leads to the side of the château.

SALVATOR

Don't budge, Roland!

(approaching the wall) Come here, Jean Taureau.

(Jean Taureau leans on the wall and holds the short ladder for Salvator, who goes up with his hands—and looks over the wall.) Loredan de Valgeneuse! The ravisher of Rose Noel—what the devil is my dear cousin doing here?

(he comes back down pensively) Where is Sac a Platre?

JEAN TAUREAU

I saw him glide down that alley. He wanted to hear or see something.

SALVATOR

Nothing upsetting in any case, since Roland didn't budge.

JEAN TAUREAU

Wait.

(he goes down the alley and makes a sign to Salvator not to budge) Here's someone coming.

SAC A PLATRE

I heard the noise of a carriage.

SALVATOR

Well?

SAC A PLATRE

It stopped at the gate. The gate opened. Two women got out and went into the château.

SALVATOR

The windows are lighting up.

JEAN TAUREAU

The devil! This may hinder our investigation.

SALVATOR

It isn't like at this time of night they will go for a walk in the garden. Never mind. Where is your carriage?

SAC A PLATRE

A hundred feet from here—under the Godeau bridge, guarded by Toussaint.

SALVATOR

You have some ropes?

SAC A PLATRE and JEAN TAUREAU

Yes.

SALVATOR

Your masks?

SAC A PLATRE and JEAN TAUREAU

Yes.

SALVATOR

You are convinced what we are doing is right?

SAC A PLATRE and JEAN TAUREAU

Yes.

SALVATOR

And whatever I order you to do, you are disposed to obey me?

SAC A PLATRE and JEAN TAUREAU

Blindly!

SALVATOR

Then in God's care!—let's get Pirolet—wait, what's Roland doing?

JEAN TAUREAU

He's scratching the earth, there, behind this bush at the foot of the tree.

SAC A PLATRE

He's whining.

SALVATOR

What's wrong my good Roland?

(Roland scratches harder) Hunt, my dog, hunt!

(calling) Sac a Platre.

(Sac a Platre approaches.)

SALVATOR

The other child was a little boy, right?

SAC A PLATRE

Yes—his name was Victor.

SALVATOR

You've never mentioned that they found his body.

SAC A PLATRE

No, Mr. Salvator, the authorities have not yet found his body.

SALVATOR

Well—we are luckier. The cadaver is there. Come Roland! Roland come.

JEAN TAUREAU

Mr. Salvator—I am a man who never fears anybody. Well, word of Jean Taureau, I am trembling like a child.

SALVATOR

Why not? I am trembling, too.

(noise of a scream) What is this again?

JEAN TAUREAU

Someone screamed.

SAC A PLATRE

A woman!

ROSE NOEL

(in the distance) Help—help—help!

SALVATOR

It's Rose Noel's voice!

ROSE NOEL

Help—come to me! I am dying!

SALVATOR

Rose, come to me! This way. Hold Roland, you two—

(the two men restrain Roland by his collar) This way, Rose, it's me, Salvator!

ROSE NOEL

(entering, pale, out of breath) Salvator, my friend! Help me, protect me! Save me!

SALVATOR

From whom? From what? I will defend you against whoever you wish.

ROSE NOEL

Mr. Gérard! My father! Orsola! They brought me to this cursed house. Save me! Save me!

VOICE OF LOREDAN

Rose! Dear Rose! What's wrong with you? Don't you know that I love you and that I respect you?

ROSE NOEL

He's coming! He's coming! Where can I hide?

SALVATOR

It's him, it's Loredan! Fear nothing!

(to Sac a Platre and Jean Taureau) Hold Roland! Put on your masks. Get the rope ready. And obey me as you promised to do.

SAC A PLATRE and JEAN TAUREAU

We are ready.

SALVATOR

Have no fear, Rose.

ROSE NOEL

Oh! Near you, I fear nothing.

LOREDAN

(hunting for Rose) Rose Noel! My dear Rose! Where are you?

SALVATOR

Over here, sir!

LOREDAN

Salvator! What have you come here for?

SALVATOR

You see, sir, I am come to look for Rose Noel who you carried off.

LOREDAN

I find you here in a garden, which is my property, you have climbed the walls like a bandit. I will treat you like a bandit.

(He draws a pistol from his pocket and intends to fire on Salvator. Rose Noel covers him with her body.)

SALVATOR

And I, I treat you as a madman. Take this man.

(Jean Taureau and Sac a Platre hurl themselves on him.)

SALVATOR

Gag him!

SALVATOR

Tie him! Is it done?

SAC A PLATRE and JEAN TAUREAU

Yes.

LOREDAN

Oh! You wretch!

SALVATOR

In the house you know, near the Cour de France, you will hide the gentlemen from sight for forty-eight hours and not let him leave. There are provisions there for three days. Go!

JEAN TAUREAU

(putting Loredan on his shoulder) Come, my dear sir.

(Sac a Platre and Jean Taureau go over the wall carrying Loredan.)

ROSE NOEL

Salvator!

SALVATOR

Dear child!

ROSE NOEL

Oh, my God, how did you get here? Who brought you here?

SALVATOR

Providence! A miracle! God who doesn't want the innocent to be punished instead of the guilty. But let's not waste time. It's my job to ask the questions and yours to reply.

ROSE NOEL

Ask—I will tell you everything, everything.

SALVATOR

Hear, in my breast, in my arms, you have no fear, right?

ROSE NOEL

No, and I am very happy!

SALVATOR

It was here in this house you were brought up, right?

ROSE NOEL

Yes, with my poor brother.

SALVATOR

You are the niece of Mr. Gérard?

ROSE NOEL

(trembling) Yes.

SALVATOR

Don't be afraid! Don't tremble! You have nothing to fear now. He had a housekeeper named Orsola? I told you not to be afraid.

ROSE NOEL

Yes.

SALVATOR

Well, now, on May 20th, 1820, what happened?

ROSE NOEL

Hold me to you, Salvator!

SALVATOR

Speak, child. On each of your trembling words hangs the life of a man. You remember everything, right?

ROSE NOEL

Oh, I do indeed. I don't think what happened in the afternoon would have happened but for a letter brought earlier.

SALVATOR

It announced the death of your father.

ROSE NOEL

Towards four o'clock in the afternoon, Mr. Sarranti returned, very pale, very agitated. He spoke for a short while with Mr. Gérard, then got on his horse with Jean, and both of them left at a gallop.

SALVATOR

Because he stole a hundred thousand shillings and murdered your brother?

ROSE NOEL

Not for that! Others did it.

SALVATOR

Gérard and Orsola?

ROSE NOEL

Yes.

SALVATOR

(turning his eyes to heaven) I knew it! Continue.

ROSE NOEL

We had dinner, Victor and me on the terrace, then they sent the gardener to Morsang! After dinner, Mr. Gérard took his rifle and led my brother to hunt.

SALVATOR

Continue—

ROSE NOEL

I really wanted to go with him. I was afraid to stay alone with Orsola, for I had seen her place a knife on the table.

SALVATOR

I am listening.

ROSE NOEL

She led me off by force. I was afraid; I cried. And then passing in front of a window that gave on the lake.

SALVATOR

Courage. Go on!

ROSE NOEL

Oh it was so terrible I can see it.

SALVATOR

You see Mr. Gérard, who was drowning your brother, right?

ROSE NOEL

(eyes fixed as if she were seeing it again) Yes! Yes! There! I called for help and at the same time, I felt a wound in my throat,

I was blinded by my blood. I called Brésil. Brésil by good luck broke his chain and ran, he got in, I don't know how—coming through the door, he leapt for Orsola's throat, who in her turn uttered a scream. I felt her hands release me. I escaped. The park's gate was closed. I got through a hole.

SALVATOR

The same without doubt which Roland passed through?

ROSE NOEL

I ran, I ran, I was mad with terror. I must have run two or three leagues. Then I stopped at a great highway where a carriage had stopped. It was that of Brocanti. She saw me, covered with blood—nearly fainting, dying, I cried to her "Hide me—hide me." She hid me in her carriage. You know the rest, right?

SALVATOR

Right up to the day you were kidnapped by Mr. de Valgeneuse. Now, I understand your joy and astonishment, in meeting Roland or rather Brésil, your emotion at the name of the Mr. Sarranti, your fright at those of Mr. Gérard and Orsola. Only, you have to tell me how you got here.

ROSE NOEL

I myself hardly know. The night I was kidnapped I came down with a fever and was delirious. Mr. Loredan was obliged to stop in a town, I don't know where—when I came to myself, it was his sister who was near my bed.

SALVATOR

Suzanne?

ROSE NOEL

Yes—she told me I had nothing to fear from her brother, that I had to pardon the violence of the passion which I had inspired in him. That he didn't want to make me his mistress but his wife. I replied to her that wife or mistress, I would never belong to him. Mr. de Valgeneuse had never come back to see me—only each day his sister received a letter which she read to me, which was full of his passion for me. Succumbing to fatigue believing they had taken me far from Paris, I was sleeping when the carriage stopped at the door of the château. I got up, hardly awake, and they left me in a room. At first I did not recognize this room, the furnishings were different. I found myself in the midst of an elegance which was unfamiliar to me. But little by little, my memories returned and with them, an unspeakable terror. I was in a house of murder! After seven years, chance fatally brought me back to the same place I had left. I opened the door and I recognized the room where Orsola tried to murder me and was herself killed. I opened the window and I recognized the lake where my poor brother perished. It was in this moving moment that another door opened and Mr. de Valgeneuse appeared. Then it was more than fear, terror, fright—it was madness. I rose to the heights, screaming "Help, help!" You heard me. Your voice guided me—I came to you—I hurled myself in your arms—! Now, you are here, I don't fear anyone. What is there to say—? What is to be done? Where must one go? My dear savior, I will listen to you and obey you.

SALVATOR

Oh—my beloved child—an atheist who heard your story would be forced to fall to his knees and say "My God! I believe you." But you said, I think that Miss Suzanne de Valgeneuse accompanied you?

ROSE NOEL

Yes.

SALVATOR

Where is she?

ROSE NOEL

(pointing to the château) She is there.

SALVATOR

That's good. I have a score to settle with her. I am going there.

ROSE NOEL

And me?

SALVATOR

You are going to stay here.

ROSE NOEL

I would never dare.

SALVATOR

And if I give you a guardian as sure as myself?

ROSE NOEL

Who?

SALVATOR

Brésil.

ROSE NOEL

Where is he?

SALVATOR

There.

ROSE NOEL

Brésil?

SALVATOR

(excitedly) Don't go. Sit there at the foot of this tree—Brésil!

ROSE NOEL

Brésil!

(Brésil comes slowly.)

SALVATOR

Brésil. Protect Leonie, and think that you will answer to me for her.

(The dog lies at her feet head on her knees.)

SALVATOR

Wait for me—both of you—innocence and fidelity, under the

protection of the Lord.

ROSE NOEL

(arms toward him) Salvator!

SALVATOR

I will return or I will call you.

ROSE NOEL

And we will wait.

(Salvator goes. Rose Noel leans her head on the dog.)

CURTAIN

ACT IV
SCENE 8

*Same as in Prologue only the furnishings and tapestries are
new.*

SUZANNE

(on the balcony, alone) I see nothing. I hear nothing. Decidedly
nothing will tame this little savage! But I hope Loredan won't
fail. It's well worth the trouble. A fortune of four or five millions!
For certain, this little girl is in love with someone. Who could
she love? An individual of her class—some gypsy. Ah, I hear
some steps. Is it you, my brother?

SALVATOR

(enters) No, it's me, cousin.

SUZANNE

Mr. Salvator!

SALVATOR

Say Conrad! Didn't we recognize each other at Pétrus' studio
at first glance?

SUZANNE

I thought you were dead, sir!

SALVATOR

In effect, I am.

SUZANNE

Then I'm having business with a ghost.

SALVATOR

Or something like.

SUZANNE

How I detest enigmas and love plain talk. Who are you? What do you want?

SALVATOR

I am a man who has believed for a long time that you had a heart, Suzanne, and who believing this, loved you madly.

SUZANNE

And did you rise from the grave to tell me that?

SALVATOR

No, I tell you this in passing—something that is in the past.

SUZANNE

Then, you no longer love me?

SALVATOR

I have that happiness. You ask me who I am and what I want. I came here precisely to tell you that.

SUZANNE

Will it be that long?

SALVATOR

Long enough for you to take a seat if you are afraid of tiring yourself.

SUZANNE

And you?

SALVATOR

I'll stand up, if you like.

SUZANNE

This story ought to be curious.

SALVATOR

And full of interest, I swear to you.

SUZANNE

For me?

SALVATOR

Especially for you.

SUZANNE

Even if, following the example you have given me, I no longer love you?

SALVATOR

You will always love your fortune and your position, two things which only I can take from you.

SUZANNE

You can take away my fortune and my position? Ridiculous!

SALVATOR

You will permit me to prove it to you?

SUZANNE

By all means!

SALVATOR

I am the natural son of the Marquis de Valgeneuse.

SUZANNE

The biological son—but not recognized.

SALVATOR

Unfortunately for you.

SUZANNE

Why's that?

SALVATOR

As a natural son, he could not leave me, if I was recognized, more than a fifth of his fortune. As non-recognized, he could leave me everything.

SUZANNE

By will.

SALVATOR

You understand.

SUZANNE

With much more facility, but he left no will.

SALVATOR

He left no will?

SUZANNE

No.

SALVATOR

The rumor is he had two. One which he dictated to his notary, Mr. Barrateau, and one which was shut in his desk.

SUZANNE

As I recall, neither one was found.

SALVATOR

In this manner, my father dying intestate, his fortune went to your father and consequently to you.

SUZANNE

At which time, my father offered you an income of six thousand francs.

SALVATOR

Which I refused.

SUZANNE

With a dignity that everyone admired.

SALVATOR

Yes, but what I supported with less dignity than the loss of my fortune was the loss of your love. Without you, who for more than two years I regarded as my life's companion, life appeared to me impossible. I decided to kill myself.

SUZANNE

I am pleased to see you gave up that resolution.

SALVATOR

Not completely, since, not being killed, I am no less dead because of it.

SUZANNE

Now that you will have to explain to me.

SALVATOR

I am going to do it briefly. I went to buy the ammunition necessary to blow my brains out. Good fortune caused me to pass before St. Roch, and the idea came to me to address one last prayer to God. A monk was preaching against suicide. In the midst of a number of listeners, an errand-boy listened to the monk. At this monk's words, I felt remorse born in my heart, and ready to die, I resolved to live in another form. I was without any resources. I knew no job nor trade—I must live by my own strength. I questioned the errand-boy and what he told me of his job pleased me. Only, so that I could break with my old friends, all the world must believe me dead. I had often studied anatomy at the Hotel Dieu, I said I wanted to study a body at home—I got a medic that I knew to let me have a subject—I hid it in my bed—I wrote a letter in which I declared I had decided to kill myself—and I asked those who found my body not to accuse anyone of my death and I discharged my pistol in the face of the one I wanted buried in my place. All happened as I planned; a doctor attested to my suicide, and seated on my errand-boy's cushions I watched my own funeral.

SUZANNE

And I had the naivety to cry for you with hot tears.

SALVATOR

You are very kind.

SUZANNE

But all that tells me nothing to the point, dear cousin; how you can dispossess me of my fortune and my position?

SALVATOR

Do you believe in Providence, my beautiful cousin?

SUZANNE

I have my days.

SALVATOR

Well, I am going to tell you a little anecdote which will make you understand why I believe it.

SUZANNE

Speak! You have no idea the interest with which I am listening to you.

SALVATOR

Well, listen to what I am going to tell you then, and don't let a word escape you. One day when I was practicing my business as errand-boy, I took a letter to a merchant of bric-à-brac in the

Rue de la Paix, and while waiting for a response to my letter, I looked over his old boxes and saw an old desk of rosewood which struck me as familiar and I recognized a little desk which once belonged to my father.

SUZANNE

You mean to say to the Marquis de Valgeneuse.

SALVATOR

Excuse me, I always make that mistake—it's only habit. A sort of filial piety caused me to purchase this furniture and it cost me twice what it is worth, but as I had had a good day's work, I bought it and brought it home where I amused myself by looking it over very carefully. I recalled then that there was a double bottomed drawer, but this secret was very well hidden, something I learned from my father, excuse me, the Marquis. Well, I found the opening and the drawer opened—can you imagine what I found?

SUZANNE

How do you expect me to imagine that?

SALVATOR

You're right—well I found the copy of the will made by Mr. Barrateau which had been lost and vainly searched for—and whose loss was the cause of my ruin and your fortune.

SUZANNE

(stupefied) You found it again?

SALVATOR

Oh! My God, yes, that will.

SUZANNE

How long ago was it?

SALVATOR

A year—a little more.

SUZANNE

This is impossible.

SALVATOR

And why?

SUZANNE

In a year, you'd have had your rights evaluated.

SALVATOR

To what good?

SUZANNE

Well, if only, not to stay an errand-boy all your life.

SALVATOR

I love my job.

SUZANNE

What! You prefer to carry letters for ten sous and packages for twenty, than to have a two hundred thousand francs income?

SALVATOR

I don't just carry letter and packages.

SUZANNE

What do you do then?

SALVATOR

A host of other things which amuse me. As for example at this moment.

SUZANNE

Well?

SALVATOR

I am recovering a young woman that your brother carried off.

SUZANNE

Ah!

SALVATOR

And whom I have taken back from him.

SUZANNE

From my brother?

SALVATOR

From your brother.

SUZANNE

From Loredan?

SALVATOR

From Loredan.

SUZANNE

And he let you do it so easily?

SALVATOR

No, oh, he drew a gun on me.

SUZANNE

And—

SALVATOR

And he lost.

SUZANNE

Come on!

SALVATOR

You always disbelieve what I tell you.

SUZANNE

Certainly, I doubt it.

SALVATOR

(opening the window) Well—look—there—down there at the foot of the tree. In the ray of moonlight. Do you see Rose Noel with Brésil who is guarding her?

SUZANNE

Where is my brother?

SALVATOR

He is—

(laughing) He is where I put those I don't want to disturb me.

SUZANNE

And you are not afraid to attack us this way?

SALVATOR

Since I found the will, I've become very audacious!

SUZANNE

(after a moment of silent rage) I would really like to see this will!

SALVATOR

Could it really be true you have this desire?

SUZANNE

Very seriously.

SALVATOR

Oh dear cousin, it will never be said that on the day I had the good fortune to find you again, you had a desire which I could fulfill and did not.

SUZANNE

You have this will on you?

SALVATOR

A will worth four million is worth keeping about—especially when it has been lost for nearly two years.

(he pulls a portfolio from his pocket) You know the Marquis' handwriting, right, dear cousin?

SUZANNE

Without doubt, I know it.

SALVATOR

(putting the paper before her eyes) Well look: "This is my Last Will and Testament written in my own handwriting, a copy of which is in the possession of Mr. Barrateau, notary, Rue de Bac No. 31—signed by Marquis de Valgeneuse."

SUZANNE

And you've shown this paper to Loredan?

SALVATOR

Oh! No! I reserved it first for you. I don't know if this attention will please your brother, dear cousin, but I can give you
my word of honor that you are the first person who has seen
it—after me.

SUZANNE

And to what end do you show it to me?

SALVATOR

Only to make you understand that you have all sorts of reasons
to be nice to me. That is, of course, dear cousin, to be set down
to revenge.

SUZANNE

And your desire that I be nice to you goes to the point of—?

SALVATOR

Goes to assure that something is happening—if you do me
the services I have come to ask you—goes to assure you of a
million under this will.

SUZANNE

And, if not?

SALVATOR

And if not, I will take the value of the will in its entirety, and keep the four million for myself. But, believe it, from a friend, accept the million and do me the service.

SUZANNE

What is my guaranty?

SALVATOR

My word of honor.

SUZANNE

What are you doing?

SALVATOR

I see that you accept.

SUZANNE

And then?

SALVATOR

(ringing) And now, I am ringing.

SUZANNE

Why?

SALVATOR

To put the horses to the carriage.

A SERVANT

(entering) Madame rang?

SUZANNE

Yes. Harness up!

(Servant leaves)

Where am I going?

SALVATOR

To Paris.

SUZANNE

And at Paris, what will I do?

SALVATOR

You will go to the Prefect of police and request a promotion for
Mr. Jackal.

SUZANNE

Why the promotion of Mr. Jackal? I thought he was your enemy?

SALVATOR

That's exactly the way I deal with my enemies. To one I give a million, to the other advancement. Only, this promotion must be given to Mr. Jackal by noon tomorrow and he must leave Paris by two o'clock. Have you something against Mr. Jackal, my beautiful cousin?

SUZANNE

On the contrary, he rendered my brother and myself a service at Madame Desmarest's, which I must reward, in supposing his intention be taken for fact, but it astonishes me you pay a million for a service I would have done for nothing.

SALVATOR

It was the only way I had of offering it to you.

SERVANT

(returning) Madame's carriage is ready.

(Suzanne takes a step to the door but returns, looking fixedly at Salvator.)

SUZANNE

So, you no longer love me, Conrad?

SALVATOR

(laughing) Oh, dear cousin, how can you ask such a question of a man who blew out his brains for you?

SUZANNE

Decidedly, I was stupid, Mr. Jackal will have his promotion before noon tomorrow.

SALVATOR

And you, dear cousin, you will have your million on the day you marry.

SUZANNE

Goodbye, cousin.

(Suzanne leaves.)

SALVATOR

(alone) She's a very intelligent woman, my cousin de Valgeneuse, but I doubt she will ever make her husband happy. She's gone. Bon Voyage! Now let's call Rose Noel.

(opens window) Rose! Rose! Come my child.

ROSE NOEL

(outside) Here we are! Come, Brésil! Come!

SALVATOR

Poor child. I understand what fear she must have had. For her, this house is full of ghosts.

(pointing to the room in which Orsola had been killed) Here, Orsola's—

(pointing to the lake) There that of her brother. If she had known down there that she was sitting ten paces from the ditch where little Victor was—here she is.

ROSE NOEL

Brésil—come, Brésil—don't leave me.

SALVATOR

Rest easy, my child. Neither Brésil nor I will ever leave you again.

ROSE NOEL

Oh—then I will be very happy.

SALVATOR

But you must be brave. You mustn't let these terrors prevent the truth from leaving your mouth. What you told me—that Mr. Gérard was guilty and Mr. Sarranti innocent. It must be said again, publicly to the whole world. What you told me of the murder your brother by his uncle and of your murder by Orsola—it must be repeated to the justices. The justices, you see, are delegates of the Lord on earth and you cannot lie to God's judges.

ROSE NOEL

Oh, I will never lie, I will be courageous, I will tell everything, I will tell all. Besides, I know that you are there to help me, to encourage me, to protect me. With you, near to you, and even far from you, now that I have found you, I fear nothing.

SALVATOR

Come, I have a sure place to hide you.

(Mr. Jackal appears.)

MR. JACKAL

Why hide the young lady—doesn't she have a natural protector in Mr. Gérard, her uncle?

SALVATOR

Mr. Jackal.

ROSE NOEL

What is this man talking about, my good friend?

MR. JACKAL

I am saying, Miss, that you owe thanks to Mr. Salvator for the trouble he has taken to get you from your ravisher, Mr. Loredan de Valgeneuse, but you see, he got here a few minutes ahead of me. Would you please follow me?

ROSE NOEL

But I don't wish to leave Mr. Salvator. I don't want to! I don't want to!

(She hugs Salvator.)

MR. JACKAL

Mr. Salvator, be good enough to make this child understand,

since she appears to me to have the greatest confidence in you, that as neither her husband nor her brother, nor her relative, you can not claim the right to protect her. That right belongs to her nearest relative after her father, that right belongs to her uncle, Mr. Gérard. Come Miss!

ROSE NOEL

Never! Never! Help me, Salvator, help me!

MR. JACKAL

The law does not discuss, Miss, it demands, and you have in Mr. Salvator a very wise advisor who will tell you to obey it without delay or rebellion.

SALVATOR

(to Jackal) Mr. Jackal, are you the bearer of a decree which orders the young lady to be returned to the hands of her uncle?

MR. JACKAL

Here it is, Mr. Salvator.

SALVATOR

(after having glanced at the paper) Obey, my child! But fear nothing, I watch over you and were you in the claws of Satan, by the living God, I will tear you from them.

CURTAIN

ACT V
SCENE 9

Gérard's room—same decorations as Scene 6.

At the rise, Gérard is occupied arranging sacks of gold in a suitcase. Someone knocks at the door. He shuts the suitcase and the door of the hiding place.

GÉRARD

Who is it?

LUDOVIC

(outside) Me, the doctor.

GÉRARD

Come in, dear Mr. Ludovic.

LUDOVIC

On your feet! And opening the door by yourself. Do you know you are sound without looking so? Without doubt, as I told you the first day I saw you, when you were apparently in so much pain. It wasn't a serious wound, but you had lost a devilish lot of blood. It's true that with good bouillon and roast beef, the blood would come back rapidly. How many days since your accident took place?

GÉRARD

Nine days today.

LUDOVIC

Well, at the end of nine days, it's fine! Continue and if you wish to follow my advice in two or three weeks, you will take a little trip which will put you completely right.

GÉRARD

I was just about to leave, my dear, sir, when this horrible misfortune happened to me—and I have my passport ready to travel.

LUDOVIC

Go to Italy, then Mr. Gérard, go to Italy. Is there nothing to keep you in Paris?

GÉRARD

Nothing.

LUDOVIC

No children?

GÉRARD

No children.

LUDOVIC

No nieces? No nephews?

GÉRARD

No.

LUDOVIC

Millionaire?

GÉRARD

People say so, but—

LUDOVIC

You, you needn't hide anything from me, it is not my fees that will ruin you. One hundred sous per visit, it's a nice price and still if you find it too expensive, I won't come back. At present, you are cured, my dear sir. Only, don't forget you won't always have such luck.

GÉRARD

On the contrary, come back, come back, as much as you like. No, your visits not only cure me, they make me feel good.

LUDOVIC

The Devil! Don't go around saying that; you will do me harm. A feel-good doctor cannot be a serious physician. And now, by my word, I am going to leave you in good company. Here's Mr. Jackal, who is probably coming to tell you he has caught your assailant. It's all the same, but it must pain you when you read, as was said in the papers, that you were dead. Mr. Jackal, you know that I am one of your admirers.

MR. JACKAL

I return the compliment, sir, for you have accomplished a magnificent cure you know.

LUDOVIC

(joking) Have you found the woman?

MR. JACKAL

If she has not been found, she will be.

LUDOVIC

Let's hope so!

(He leaves singing.)

MR. JACKAL

You have a charming doctor there, Mr. Gérard.

GÉRARD

Yes, and I told him just now I am always happier after he leaves me.

MR. JACKAL

Well, I bring you news which will make you happier still.

GÉRARD

Really?

MR. JACKAL

But take the trouble to have a seat, you are still weak.

(Gérard sits) Since I've known you, dear Mr. Gérard, I have noticed in you a bit of sadness, melancholy and taciturnity.

GÉRARD

The fact is I'm not gay.

MR. JACKAL

I said to myself, "There's no sadness without some reason."

(Gérard sighs) Well, what makes this brave Mr. Gérard sad is the death of his nephew, Victor, and the disappearance of his niece, Leonie. His nephew one cannot bring back to him, but his niece can be found again.

GÉRARD

(shaking his head) I have done all I could to achieve this result and I have not succeeded.

MR. JACKAL

Because you do not have at your disposition the means that I have. Also, I've been luckier than you.

GÉRARD

(frightened) Luckier than me! What have you done then?

MR. JACKAL

I've done some research.

GÉRARD

(paling) You?

MR. JACKAL

Yes, and—

GÉRARD

(with a voice out of breath) And?

MR. JACKAL

And I have found her.

GÉRARD

Who?

MR. JACKAL

Leonie, your niece!

GÉRARD

My God!

MR. JACKAL

Come on, good! You're going to be sick with joy now—Ah, dear Mr. Gérard, you have a very tender heart.

GÉRARD

And where is she?

MR. JACKAL

Below in the carriage. She's only waiting for your permission to throw herself in your arms.

GÉRARD

Oh!

MR. JACKAL

(to the wings) Mr. Gérard says he cannot resist his impatience— have Miss Leonie come up.

(Gérard gets up and goes trembling to the room at the rear) Where are you going?

GÉRARD

I don't know.

MR. JACKAL

My dear Mr. Gérard, you don't seem to be completely right in your head and therefore you won't object that an officer of the government takes some precautions. A single moment of madness can sometimes cause irreparable damage. I bring you back your niece, Leonie. She's a beautiful girl of sixteen, so beset by misfortune that from the moment I received the order placing her back in your hands, she inspired in me the liveliest interest and I tell you, my dear Mr. Gérard, it's in your care that this charming girl is placed. Well, take care nothing bad happens to her, watch that a single hair doesn't fall from her head, for wherever you may be, even in a foreign country, even in America, even in China, I will reach out my arm and bring you to me—and then, you know the old adage—tooth for tooth, eye for eye—head for head—! But what's wrong with you? You are not listening to me. What I am now saying has its importance.

GÉRARD

(eye fixed on the door) Mr. Jackal! Mr. Jackal! Do you see—!

MR. JACKAL

Certainly, I see! I see your niece entering and I am withdrawing to leave you all the pleasure of seeing her again. Goodbye, Mr. Gérard! Goodbye Miss.

(to gendarmes) Gentlemen, you have nothing to do here.

(Stops at the most distant part of the room. Gérard looks at her with a profound terror. Moment of silence.)

GÉRARD

(in a voice he tries to render caressing) Leonie, my dear Leonie, is it really you?

LEONIE

Myself! And if you doubt it, look, uncle.

(she opens her collar) There's the scar from Orsola's knife!

GÉRARD

Yes, she was an evil creature, and who, to me also, did evil! But God has punished her.

LEONIE

If it was God who punished her, why, since she was the least guilty of the two, was she punished the most severely?

GÉRARD

Leonie! Leonie! Remember how much I loved you.

LEONIE

I remember that the one you loved the best was my brother Victor. Your preferences are terrible, uncle. They kill. Don't love me too much.

GÉRARD

You are right, Leonie, accuse me, overwhelm me, condemn me. Never, no never, can you say more than my conscience has said. Look at me! It's seven years since that wretched crime was committed; I have aged twenty years in seven years. It's really a terrible thing, isn't it? That you find yourself face-to-face with me in the sunlight. That to see you enter, pale and threatening in this room, and when I doubt it's you, to see you trace the scar from Orsola's knife, telling me "look." Well, less terrible I tell you, than to see in my dreams the hair running in the water of the lake and the pressed face, the ghostly sight of your poor brother crying to me, "Uncle, Uncle, good Uncle, do not kill me." But let's let the poor child sleep in his tomb. He rests there more peacefully than I do in my bed, I am sure of it—and let's concern ourselves with you, my dear Leonie—of your future, of your happiness. You are young, you are pretty, you can be happy. I don't speak of riches.

(going to the door which he opens) Hold on, this armoire contains millions—for fear of having them stolen, I created this hiding place. No one knows of it. No one can find it when it is closed; it only opens to the a touch known only to me. Some thieves came, they threatened me with death if I wouldn't tell them where my money was—I told them nothing. It was for you, Leonie, that I protected all this. For me, I have no need of it, what would I do with it? Come on, it's ready, let's leave. You see my portfolio, there is my passport. There it is. The carriage is below—at our disposal—nothing keeps us here—come Leonie, let us go.

LEONIE

I am not leaving.

GÉRARD

What do you mean, not leaving?

LEONIE

No, my testimony is necessary, I am staying.

GÉRARD

Your testimony is necessary for what?

LEONIE

So the innocent will not be condemned in place of the guilty.

GÉRARD

(almost threatening) Oh, you wish to stay to denounce me—to have me condemned—to see me on the scaffold?

LEONIE

No, but to see that Mr. Sarranti does not mount in your place.

GÉRARD

Sarranti, Sarranti. What does that man matter to you? Fate pursues him, abandon him to his fate.

LEONIE

Meaning you want me to kill him when with a word, I can save him? You want my nights to be haunted by a specter, only your ghost is merely that of a drowned child who cries, "Good uncle, don't kill me!" My ghost would be an innocent who from the height of the scaffold cried to me "Wretch, you let me die!" I don't leave.

GÉRARD

Oh—willingly or by force, it's necessary for you to leave.

LEONIE

Willingly, I have told you, I won't leave. By force, how will you do it? Will you drag me down the stairs? In the stairs, I will scream! You will shut me in a carriage. In the carriage I will scream! You'll keep me in this room. In this room there is a window and from the window, I will scream. You will take me to a desert—in the desert I will scream! And take care! In place of judges to hear me in this desert, there will be God! The man who brought me, here told you that he gave you your crime to conceal. He lied, it was your punishment.

GÉRARD

(head in his hand) Frightful logic of murder! Here I am forced, because I committed one murder. Either to submit to punishment or commit a second—Leonie!

LEONIE

(running to the window and opening it) Don't come near me or I will scream!

GÉRARD

Leonie, I am not threatening you, I am begging you.

LEONIE

Begging or threatening, sir, little matter! You are a man and you are armed. I am a child without defense, but I am much stronger, I am more invulnerable than you, because I am the truth, because I am justice, because I am the law!

GÉRARD

What is there for me to do then?

LEONIE

To open the door for me and to tell me "Go freely where your duty tells you to go" or rather—

GÉRARD

Or rather?

LEONIE

Or rather kill me, as you killed my brother.

GÉRARD

She too!

(looks around him, sees the door of the hiding place open and appears struck by an idea to himself) Well, I will not kill you. I will leave you to die.

(threatening) Leonie!

LEONIE

(opening the window) Help!

(Gérard leaps on her and throws his cloak over her)

GÉRARD

Ah, you scream!

LEONIE

(in a weakening voice) Help! Help! Murder!

GÉRARD

(drags her to the hiding place and locks her in) Scream now! We will see if, when I am gone, when all the doors are shut, we will see if someone will hear you and come open for you.

(he takes the suitcase full of gold and goes to the door, then recoils) The monk! What do you want with me?

DOMINIQUE

I am going to tell you.

GÉRARD

Not at this time, not at this moment. This evening, tomorrow, the day after.

DOMINIQUE

No, immediately.

GÉRARD

I cannot.

(Gérard goes to the door, Dominique bars his way.)

DOMINIQUE

You shall not pass.

GÉRARD

Too late! Five minutes too late!

DOMINIQUE

It is God who measures time. Will you listen to me?

GÉRARD

Speak then.

DOMINIQUE

I come to ask you the right to reveal your confession.

GÉRARD

Meaning you come to ask my death, meaning you come to lead me by the hand to the scaffold?

DOMINIQUE

No, sir, for this permission granted—to no longer oppose your departure.

GÉRARD

My departure—and after that, you denounce me, the telegraph follows me, and ten leagues, twenty leagues, thirty leagues from here, they arrest me.

DOMINIQUE

I give you my word, sir, and you know I am a slave to my word, that tomorrow at noon—meaning when you are in Belgium, I will exercise your permission.

GÉRARD

And when I am in Belgium, as there is a murder, you will obtain my extradition.

DOMINIQUE

I will not solicit it, sir. I am a man of peace. I ask only that the sinner repent and not that he be punished. I wish not that you die, but that my father not die.

GÉRARD

Impossible! You ask an impossible thing of me.

DOMINIQUE

What you are doing is terrible! At this moment, the court is deliberating the fate of my father, perhaps at this instant, they are pronouncing his sentence and the court's orders are executed in forty-eight hours.

GÉRARD

The agreement you had with me is exact, after my death, yes, but so long as I live, no, no, a thousand times no. Let me pass then. You can do nothing against me.

DOMINIQUE

(in complete despair) Sir, you know that to persuade you I have employed all means, all words, all prayers, all supplications, which can raise an echo in the heart of a man? Do you think if there was a possibility of saving my father outside of this; I would propose it to you; if there is a way, say it, I ask nothing better to use it, even if it will kill my worldly body and lose my soul in the next. Wait, I put myself at your knees to beg you to save my father. A way—indicate a way.

GÉRARD

I don't know of any! Let me pass!

DOMINIQUE

And if I kill you?

(Salvator rushes in and restrains Dominique)

SALVATOR

Stop—such a rogue doesn't deserve to die by the hand of an honest man! Help, Roland!

(Roland rushes into the room and jumps at the throat of Gérard who rolls with him behind the bed.)

GÉRARD

Protect me from the dog—and let me leave—and I will sign whatever you wish.

(Salvator pulls the dog from Gérard.)

SALVATOR

Good work, Roland!

DOMINIQUE

(taking a pen and presenting it and a manuscript to Gérard) Write! Tuesday—11 a.m. I authorize the son of Mr. Sarranti to reveal my confession, Wednesday at noon. Sign!

(Gérard signs.)

SALVATOR

And now go hang where it pleases God and human justice to adorn a gibbet! Go—go away—wretch!

DOMINIQUE

(hugging Salvator) Oh, my savior! Embrace me!

SALVATOR

Now—where is Rose Noel?

DOMINIQUE

Rose Noel? I haven't seen her.

SALVATOR

She ought to be here now. Mr. Jackal brought her here this morning. Ah—in the other room without doubt.

(he goes in) Rose Noel.

DOMINIQUE

(calling) Leonie! Leonie!

SALVATOR

(pale, frightened, reappears at the door) Rose Noel! Rose Noel! Where are you.

DOMINIQUE

My God! What are you afraid of?

SALVATOR

Everything! This man is capable of everything!

DOMINIQUE

He must have killed her to flee, just as he killed her brother.

SALVATOR

My God!

DOMINIQUE

Listen! No—I thought I heard a groan.

SALVATOR

Ah, that's her. It cannot be her last cry. Where is she, my God? Where is she?

(to Roland, who scratches the wall) What are you doing, Roland? What's wrong with him? Look, my dog—look—

(after a pause) Dead or alive, Rose Noel is there.

DOMINIQUE

Wait.

SALVATOR

Not the door! The wall. Oh—if necessary I will tear the house down to find her body. Rose Noel! Rose Noel!

DOMINIQUE

I remember a nook hollowed in the wall is where he'd hid his
gold—it's where he hid a manuscript—a spring, a secret. God
permitted that he showed it to me.

(He presses the spring, the hiding place opens—one sees Rose
Noel on her knees, suffocating, almost asphyxiated. She has,
with her teeth and her hands torn the cloak apart, through
which her head and one of her arms have broken through in the
struggle.)

SALVATOR

(taking her in his arms) Oh! Rose Noel! Living. Thanks to God!

LEONIE

Oh, Salvator, I knew it was you who saved me.

MR. JACKAL

(entering) Gentlemen! Gentlemen!

DOMINIQUE and SALVATOR

Mr. Jackal.

MR. JACKAL

Yes, Mr. Jackal in person who comes to tell you that thanks to
the influence of a powerful and unknown person he has been
named central Commissioner at Toulon.

(to Gérard, who enters) If you ever pass by there, Mr. Gérard, I
will put myself at your disposal.

SALVATOR

But how does he know that Mr. Gérard—?

MR. JACKAL

It's quite simple. Before leaving for my new destination, I came to pay a visit to Mr. Henry, my protégé. All of a sudden, I saw pass in a post chaise, Mr. Gérard, who, instead of parting with his niece as I expressly recommended, was leaving alone. I was afraid some misfortune had happened to Rose Noel, who I love very much and I brought Mr. Gérard back here to demand a little explanation.

SALVATOR

I am going to give it to you. Mr. Gérard, in leaving, had thrown his niece living into this sepulcher where she would be dead at this time had we not got her out, thanks to Brésil.

MR. JACKAL

Well—as I've always said, Mr. Salvator, cherchez la femme!

CURTAIN

ABOUT THE AUTHOR

Frank J. Morlock has written and translated many plays since retiring from the legal profession in 1992. His translations have also appeared on Project Gutenberg, the Alexandre Dumas Père web page, Literature in the Age of Napoléon, Infinite Artistries. com, and Munsey's (formerly Blackmask). In 2006 he received an award from the North American Jules Verne Society for his translations of Verne's plays. He lives and works in México.

www.ingramcontent.com/pod-product-compliance
Lightning Source LLC
Chambersburg PA
CBHW030914090426
42737CB00007B/188